AN ASTROLOGICAL
INSIGHT

AN ASTROLOGICAL INSIGHT

KAY ANDREWS

BALBOA.
PRESS
A DIVISION OF HAY HOUSE

Balboa Press books may be ordered through booksellers or by contacting:

Balboa Press
A Division of Hay House
1663 Liberty Drive
Bloomington, IN 47403
www.balboapress.com
1-(877) 407-4847

Because of the dynamic nature of the Internet, any web addresses or links contained in this book may have changed since publication and may no longer be valid. The views expressed in this work are solely those of the author and do not necessarily reflect the views of the publisher, and the publisher hereby disclaims any responsibility for them.

The author of this book does not dispense medical advice or prescribe the use of any technique as a form of treatment for physical, emotional, or medical problems without the advice of a physician, either directly or indirectly. The intent of the author is only to offer information of a general nature to help you in your quest for emotional and spiritual well-being. In the event you use any of the information in this book for yourself, which is your constitutional right, the author and the publisher assume no responsibility for your actions.

Any people depicted in stock imagery provided by Thinkstock are models, and such images are being used for illustrative purposes only.

Certain stock imagery © Thinkstock.

ISBN: 978-1-4525-8159-0 (sc)
ISBN: 978-1-4525-8160-6 (e)

Printed in the United States of America.

Balboa Press rev. date: 09/12/2013

In humble dedication to the eternal presence of
Omnipotent Will
Omnipresent Love
Omniscient Light of Life

TABLE OF CONTENTS

PREFACE

Astrology, the science and study of the stars, is one of many universal tools to personal awareness discovery. To the reader whose present exposure or knowledge of astrology is minimal, recognize that it is not necessary to know "everything" (if such were possible) to understand "something" of astrology. This book defines astrological terms with positive philosophical insight to life's implicating truths known and expressed by avatars, writers, poets, and seers through the ages.

Each Soul is a unique "one of a kind" model composed of an identifiable physical, emotional and mental body. Each physical feature, fingerprint, voice identity, DNA, emotional and mental expression is distinctive in each life. Even identical twins, may have similar life experiences, yet each will respond differently. Each soul also, has an innate spiritual body; theological and truth teachers have labeled it "guardian angel," "holy ghost," "Christ within." All of life's energy streams from One Spirit Source—One loving, guiding light.

It is the author's belief that each soul incarnates with a "pre-planned" guided purpose and intent, at the exact time and place necessary for beneficial growth to the self and others. Each individual is "programmed" (as can be seen in an astrology chart,) to meet a wide variety of experiences; some are as "moral choice tests," some, "follow the heart-love and understanding tests," some may be "karmic, unfinished business," and some meant as an "example to assist others." At times, life's experiences are painful—teaching understanding through overcoming. All experiences are meant for each life to grow in love.

There are various approaches to reading an astrology chart. Ultimately, insights are revealed from the interpreters inspired (in spirit) knowing, guiding, "still small voice within." The astrological symbolic parts, and signs defined in this book, are presented as a helpful method for the interpretation and insight into one's astrology chart-life map. May it be an aid to personal self discovery and fulfilling purpose—to "Know Thyself."

> "To be what we are, and to become what we are capable of becoming is the only end in life" Spinoza.

Acknowledgements: To Stephen Andrews and Vicky Campo with grateful appreciation for the valuable technical and graphic assistance with this book.

To my dear Albert, for his wise critique and fifty-four years of supportive love.

DEFINING THE INTERPRETIVE PARTS OF ONE'S ASTROLOGICAL MAP

1. The Astrology Chart—Individual Map
2. Astrological Houses
3. Zodiac Signs
4. Signs Applied to Houses
5. Houses and Interacting Relationships
6. Astrological Qualities
7. Astrological Elements

THE ASTROLOGY CHART—INDIVIDUAL MAP

The center of an astrology chart is the circle "**O**" symbol of un-manifested consciousness; the infinite center or source of all areas of life experience.

"God is a circle whose center is everywhere and whose circumference is nowhere" Empedocles.

One's horoscope-chart-astrological map is one's symbolic blueprint-diagram showing a view of the heavens at the moment of birth, reflecting a way to self awareness. "as above—so below."

The chart is divided and categorized into many parts (expressions) so that through the study of the various parts, one may come to know the whole. While the possible combinations are immeasurable, all parts are joined to one perfect whole. The "wholeness" of self is a part of the "wholeness" of the Source (center) from which "man lives and moves and has his being."

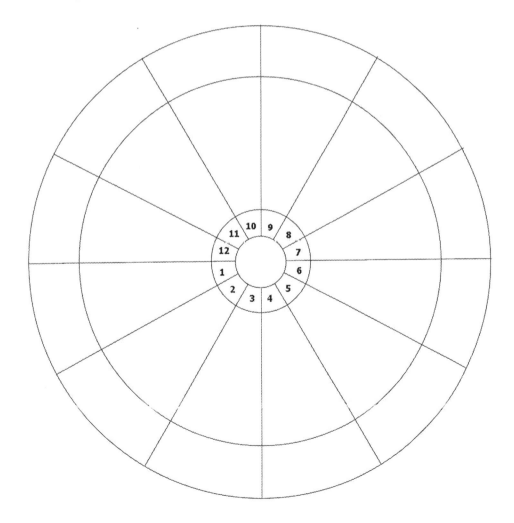

ASTROLOGICAL HOUSES

"As the sun returns in the east, so let our patience be renewed with the dawn; as the sun lightens the world, so let our loving kindness make bright the house of our habitation" Robert Louis Stevenson.

Each of the astrological Signs and Planets are expressed in one's individual Chart of Houses.

The twelve astrological houses represent fields of activity or areas of life experience, which include a wide range of interpretive representation. A general word-words will be used for descriptive application.

1. ASCENDANT—East Horizon, personal self-image, physical appearance, attitude
2. securities, possessions, expenditures, personal values, resources, assets-income
3. communications, siblings, neighbors, relatives, early education, short trips-transportation
4. NADIR—roots, past, one parent, home, real estate, beginning and end of life
5. children, creation-creativity, pleasurable affairs, sports, gambling-games, hobbies
6. service, work, employees, peers, general health, health habits, small animals
7. DESCENDENT—partnerships, marriage, council, close friendships, open conflicts
8. responsibilities, hidden mysteries, death, inheritances, taxes, partner securities, surgery
9. philosophy, religion, colleges-universities, long journeys, foreign travel, publishing, law
10. MIDHEAVEN—career goals, profession, public image-reputation, honors, one parent
11. social groups, organizations-clubs, goals-ambitions-aspirations, general friendships
12. self understandings, beliefs, visions, secrets, areas of confinement, institutions, hospitals

THE CIRCLE OF HOUSES

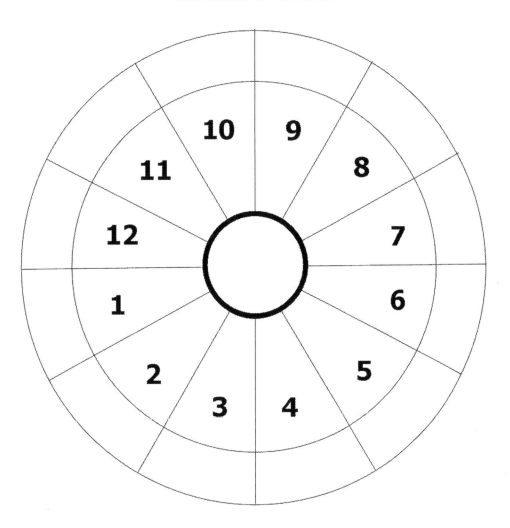

ZODIAC SIGNS

All Zodiac signs are represented in each individual's astrological chart—map
Listed are the twelve zodiac signs with some identifying characteristic words

Aries Ram—self motivated, ambition, pioneer spirit, enthusiastic, bold, assertive, leader

Taurus Bull—stable, patient, possessive, loyal, determined, practical, dependable, responsible.

Gemini Twins—versatile, witty, communicator, energetic, many interests, articulate, agile

Cancer Crab—nurturing, caring, sympathetic, possessive, giving, tenacious, shrewd, homebody

Leo Lion—regal, proud, loyal, courageous, generous, dramatic, confident, flamboyant, dignified

Virgo Virgin—refined, purity, analytical, discriminating, detailed, organized, observant, modest

Libra Scales—discreet, fair, sociable, diplomatic, fosters harmony, refined, peacemaker, poised

Scorpio Scorpion Eagle Phoenix Bird—resourceful, intense, strong willed, private, magnetic, dedicated

Sagittarius Archer—aspiring, outspoken, humorous, direct, optimistic, free spirit, easy going, logical

Capricorn Goat—industrious, traditional, disciplined, dignified, worker, conservative, serious, ambitious

Aquarius Water Bearer—humanitarian, innovative, unconventional, independent, altruistic, friendly

Pisces Fish—imaginative, mystical, intuitive, romantic, charitable, dreamer, idealistic, sensitive

SIGNS APPLIED TO HOUSES

Listed are symbolic glyphs which represent each astrological sign.

Aries	♈	Libra	♎
Taurus	♉	Scorpio	♏
Gemini	♊	Sagittarius	♐
Cancer	♋	Capricorn	♑
Leo	♌	Aquarius	♒
Virgo	♍	Pisces	♓

Signs to Houses

HOUSES INTERACTING RELATIONSHIPS

Dividing one's astrological chart into three interactive parts, gives added insight to the people and people relationships in one's life. Part two and three are mostly general category relationships—named in part.

One: Personal Houses

> First—self, me "I AM" great grandchildren
> Second—one's personal banker, stockbroker, financial advisor, jeweler
> Third—siblings, cousins, neighbors, personal teachers
> Fourth—elders, seniors, family, realtors, renters, one parent

Two: Other—One to One Houses

> Fifth—children, actors, gamblers, recreation and sports people, heart specialists, youth teachers
> Sixth—healers, doctors, nurses, druggists, employees, workers, cooks, waiters, police
> Seventh—spouse, partners, close friends, professional consultants, astrologers, public rivals
> Eighth—tax accountants, tax collectors, coroners, insurance salesmen, surgeons

Three Group—Universal Houses

> Ninth—travel agents, attorneys, clergymen, foreign people, juries, college professors, philosophers
> Tenth—bosses, supervisors, CEO's, executives, celebrities, state and government officials, one parent
> Eleventh—organizations, groups, clubs, councils, colleagues, fraternities, sororities, general friendships
> Twelfth—workers in hospitals, institutions, jails, burglars, detectives, secret service agents

Interacting Relationships

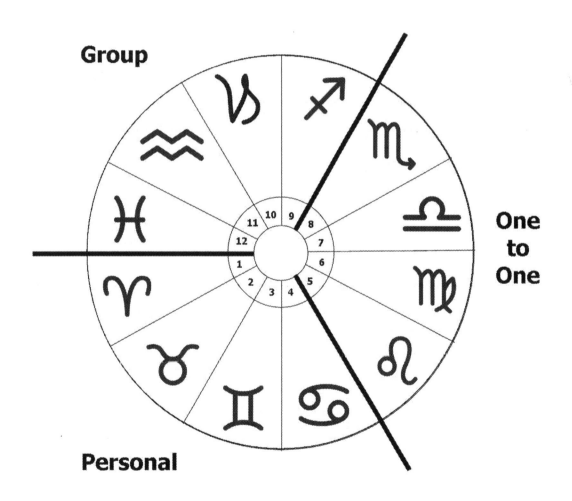

ASTROLOGICAL QUALITIES-MODALITIES

Cardinal Will   Fixed Love   Mutable Light

The Modalities of an astrology chart, of signs and houses are placed in three definitive categories of expression called Qualities. The Qualities are identified as Cardinal, Fixed and Mutable.

Based on what is known about houses and signs, the primary function or basis of each Cardinal sign is to express and manifest assertive activity of the levels and cycles of Omnipotent Will; each Succeeding Fixed Security house and sign to express and manifest the levels and cycles of Love through concentrated energy; and each Cadent Mutable sign and house to express and manifest the levels and cycles of Omniscient Light through associative adjustment. In each sign, the whole of the Source is present; and at the same time, each sign expresses in a specific way and area definable to the whole. As the body is the whole of man physically, the hand is a specific part expressing in a specific way but could not express unless it contained the entire whole within.

"Knowledge, Love, Power-there is the complete life." Henri-Frédéric Amiel Philosopher

The Cardinal Signs are: Aries, Cancer, Libra and Capricorn.
The Cardinal Houses-Angular Houses are the First, Fourth, Seventh and Tenth.

The Fixed Succeeding Security Signs are: Taurus, Leo, Scorpio and Aquarius.
Fixed Security Houses consolidate and stabilize—Second, Fifth, Eighth, and Eleventh.

The Cadent Mutable Associative Signs are Gemini, Virgo, Sagittarius, and Pisces.
The Cadent Mutable Houses are the Third, Sixth, Ninth, and Twelfth.

Qualities

C- Cardinal Will   F - Fixed Love   M - Mutable Light

QUALITIES
CARDINAL WILL

No individual has power. All power comes from one Omnipotent Source—Divine Will. The very power, the life essence—the "I AM" identity within each man is of and from that Source. We live from one Source, one life-force of Divine Will. The quality, "goodness" or "badness" use of this force as expressed in one's life, depends on individual choice. Creative Spirit, gives to man a creative spirit "made in the image and likeness" to choose to apply divinely given power in life. Man has the choice to use this power to help or harm, to heal or destroy. While one is capable of "doing" divine Will, without consciously attempting to do so; human will, (a conscious choice in action) is not capable of expanding the higher self. One's self-created barriers must be removed so that the clarity of the Will of the divine inner-Source can come through. Each individual must get his or her human ego-self out of the way; be still to the inner Source; In conscious aware, submission to divine Will Power, strength comes to the individual who is at one with his/her Source.

> "God alone speaks to us, and we wait in singleness of heart, that we may know his Will, and in the silence of our spirits, that we may do that only."
> Henry W. Longfellow

Each sign holds divine Will potential. The Cardinal Will signs exemplify and demonstrate an understanding of the Will in four areas of defined expression.

The Cardinal Will signs—**Aries, Cancer, Libra and Capricorn**, initiate assertive action activity.

The Cardinal Will angular houses—**First, Fourth, Seventh, and Tenth**, initiate change.

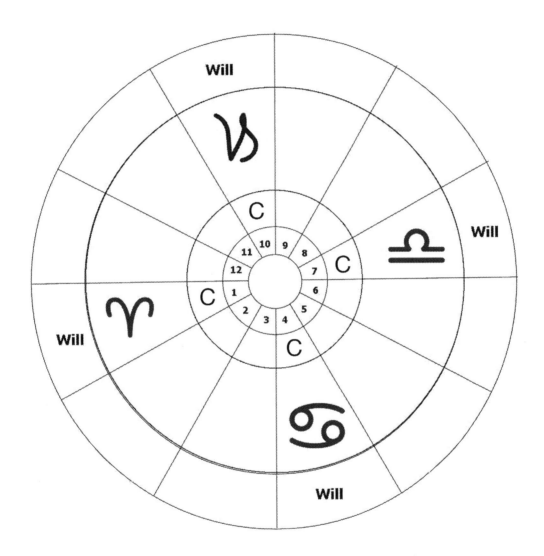

Cardinal Will

QUALITIES
FIXED LOVE

The harmony of life is love, the outpouring love force in action. The motivating power Source is Love. Love allows free expression. Love power may be freely used in a positive or negative expression. Negative use (e.g.; smothering love) brings negative results producing "good," though painful, learning experience leading to soul growth. Each person grows through all experience, pleasant or unpleasant. If power is used positively in love, one is in harmony with his/her Source in divine flow, producing good fruit of the spirit. In love flow, inner peace and contentment is realized. A joyful, living, universal rhythm is expressed in love.

"We are all born for Love; it is the principle of existence and its only end."
Benjamin Disraeli

The fixed-security signs **Taurus, Leo, Scorpio, and Aquarius** express love through concentrated energy of consolidating union and persistent purpose.

The fixed succeeding security, focused love houses are the **Second—Fifth— Eighth— Eleventh.**

Love potential is present in all signs. The fixed-security signs and houses demonstrate and exemplify the specific love relationships in expression.

Fixed Love

QUALITIES
MUTABLE—LIGHT

Light is symbolic of infinite knowledge, the creation of Omniscient mind—the constructive, illuminating activity of life. Light carries the Omnipresent, life energy functioning in human consciousness. Man in darkness is unaware of his/her own bestowed inner-illumination. As one expands in light, he/she evolves through experience to increasing awareness, consciously seeking and "seeing" with the inner knowing eye, fulfilling inherent destiny to become, in full light, a visible Sun—son of life's Source.

"the true light, which lighteth every man that cometh into the world."
Jesus-*Bible: John 1.9*

"Ye are the light of the world." Jesus—*Bible: Matt: v 14*

The mutable-light signs **Gemini, Virgo, Sagittarius, and Pisces** are associative signs of flexible adaptable, adjustment. The mutable light signs symbolically exemplify specific mental ability and keen interacting mental relationships. Light is present in all signs.

Mutable-light Associative cadent houses are the **Third, Sixth, Ninth, Twelfth**. Cadent houses are houses of transiting change.

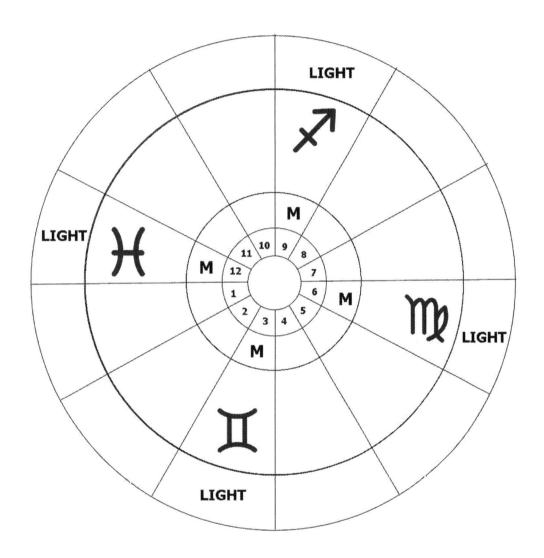

Mutable Light

ASTROLOGICAL ELEMENTS

Fire—Earth—Air—Water

Through the application of astrological insights, one can begin to understand causes behind human conduct. Man is of the elements and influenced by them. Esoterically, the elements represent bodies of expression in each man. Astrology defines these element bodies as **Fire, Earth, Air, and Water.**

All of the elements are represented in each individual. All are symbolic parts of the whole, representing the four bodies of man—spiritual, physical, mental and emotional, and are concepts abstract in nature. The elements of man—microcosm evolve from the un-manifested-Macrocosmic life Source.

"Nature stamped us in a heavenly mould" Campbell *the Mansions of Hope*

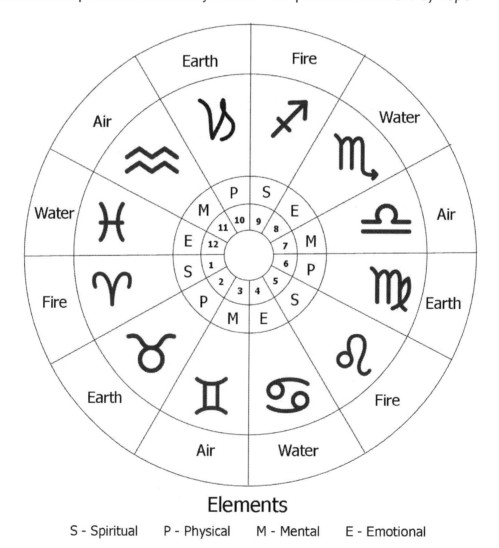

Elements

S - Spiritual   P - Physical   M - Mental   E - Emotional

ELEMENTS: FIRE—MAN'S SPIRITUAL BODY

The **Fire** signs, **Aries, Leo and Sagittarius**, fall in the **First, Fifth and Ninth** Houses of Life expressing life's dynamic energy, motivations of power and conviction. Fire signs represent expressions of man's active Spirit body—the Life Force within, an assertive impulse, with expressions of enthusiasm, vitality, intensity, and inspiration. Fire signs are a positive, outgoing Yang polarity. The inspired one is ignited in Spirit. The divine spark within ignites the spirit in man to evolving fire purification. All men are of one Spirit.

"Incorruptible Spirit is in all things." Wisdom of Solomon.
"Spirit is not external to anyone, but it is present with all things." Plotinus

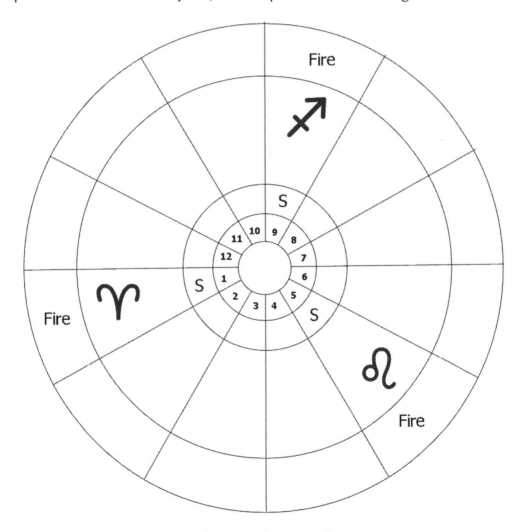

Fire - Spiritual

ELEMENTS: EARTH—MAN'S PHYSICAL BODY

The **Earth** signs, **Taurus, Virgo, and Capricorn** fall in the **Second, Eighth, and Tenth** Houses of Substance and represent functioning areas of material and/or objective activity. Earth signs instigate an ability to make tangible, useful, practical result expressions through the physical human body. Earth signs represent conservative stability, practicality, prudence, and security. Earth Signs are of a negative, receptive, Yin polarity. Earth signs help to develop the goal of each one, to manifest and project the divine essence of life in physical expression.

"There is a divinity within our breast." Ovid
"For the soul the body form doth take, for Soul is form, and doth the body make."
Spencer

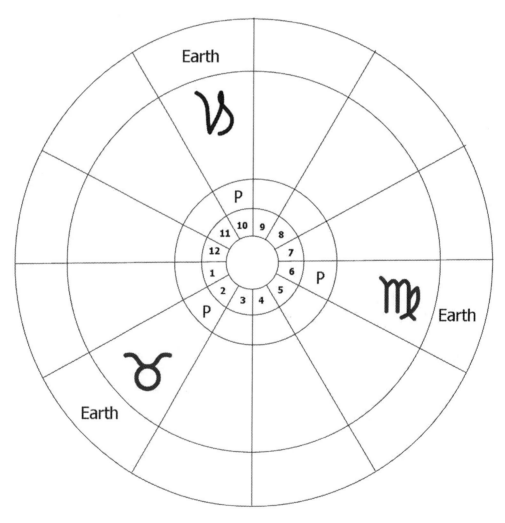

Earth - Physical

ELEMENTS: AIR—MAN'S MENTAL BODY

The **Air** signs, **Gemini, Libra and Aquarius**, function in the **Third, Seventh, and Eleventh** Houses of Associations to symbolically express mental associations as abstract play with ideas, intellectual activity, and idealism. Air signs teach discipline of thought processes and expression. Air signs focus on relationships, communications, intellectual pursuits, and socializing. Air Signs are of a positive, outgoing Yang polarity.

The human mental body goal is to consciously align one's mind and thoughts with Omniscient divine mind.

"There is one mind common to all individual men" Emerson

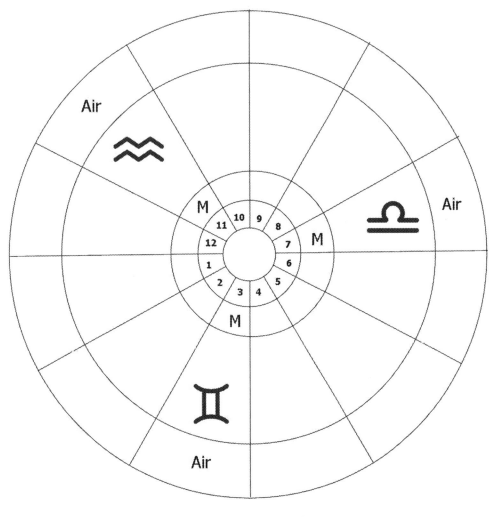

Air - Mental

ELEMENTS: WATER—MAN'S EMOTIONAL BODY

The **Water** signs, **Cancer, Scorpio and Pisces**, fall in the **Fourth, Eighth and Twelfth** Houses of Endings. Man's emotional bodies represent the psychic or subjective phases of human nature; representing one's psychological, emotional desire body. Water Signs are compassionate, emotional, impressionable, and intuitive.

Water signs are a negative-receptive Yin polarity; teaching refinement of sensitivity through emotional experiences. When one's outer emotional expression is open to, and guided from an inner divine nature, one is in composed harmony within the self and with others.

"The highest motive is to be like Water: Water is essential to all living things, yet it demands no pay or recognition. Rather it flows humbly to the lowest level. Nothing is weaker than Water. Yet for overcoming what is hard and strong nothing surpasses it." Tau Te Ching:

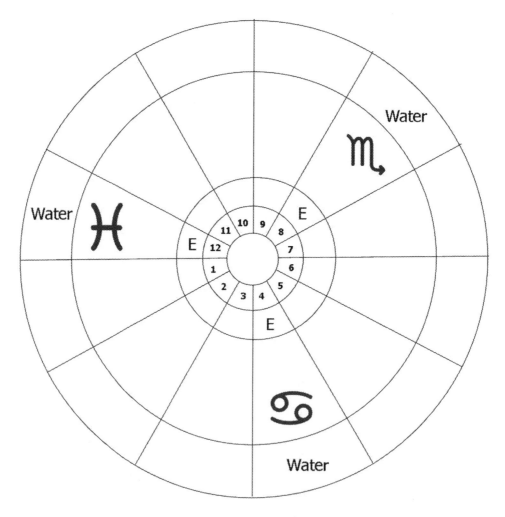

Water - Emotional

PLANETARY RULERSHIPS TO SIGNS INTERPRETED

1. Defining Planet Body Rulers
2. Ancient Past Sign Rulers
3. Modern Sign Rulers Added
4. New Age Ruling Influences
5. Planetary Rulers—Co Rulers
6. Exaltation Rulers
7. Rulers—Co-Rulers—Exaltation Rulers
8. The Planets Applied
9. About Detriment and Fall Rulers
10. About Astrological Aspects

DEFINING PLANET BODY RULERS

"It is the stars, the stars above us, govern our conditions." Shakespeare.

Planetary bodies symbolically represent the directing of universal energies through astrological signs or channels of expression and through insightful reflection of the corresponding "one in all"—"as above so below" All of life's energy comes from one universal Source. Divine law is the logical process by which the Source manifests.

"man is ever in the presence of an infinite and eternal energy from which all things proceed." Herbert Spencer

Astrological signs represent channels through which directed planetary energies flow to bring qualities of experience.

Each planetary body is a Ruler, a Co-Ruler, and an Exaltation Ruler to some sign. All of the ruling planets fall in absolute order in the heavens. Each planetary body rules or co-rules a projecting positive masculine astrological sign and a negative receptive feminine sign.

A Ruling-Planet denotes a natural expression of energy in harmony with its sign; generally interpreted on a conscious-exoteric, functional level.

A Co-Ruling Planet denotes an affinity or related harmonious energy to its sign; generally assisting an exoteric level of understanding of interpretation.

An Exalting Planet symbolizes the highest potential goal of expression from the exalted ruler to its sign; generally interpreted on an esoteric higher inner-level direction to consciousness adaptation.

The sign in which a planet attains its greatest influence is in the sign of exaltation.

PLANET SYMBOLS

Planets are symbolically composed of three basic glyphs

✝ The Cross of material earth

☽ The Moon of personality

○ The Circle (Sun) of spirit

Planetary bodies with general astrological identifying words:

⊙ Sun—spirit, vital power, individuality, ego identity, character potential

☽ Moon—personality, habits, instincts, psyche, soul

☿ Mercury—communicator, coordinator, messenger, intellect

♀ Venus—harmony, sensory feeling, love emotions, beauty, sociability

♂ Mars—initiates action, directed energy, drive, warrior, demonstration

♃ Jupiter—expansion, growth, achievement, optimism, benefic

♄ Saturn—structure, responsibility, character building, refinement, restrictions

♅ Uranus—awareness, freedom, disruptive, innovative, change, revolution

♆ Neptune—intuitive, sensitivity, illusion, visionary, insights, imagination

♇ Pluto—regeneration, renewal, new-birth, upheaval, transformation

X Personal inner-love connection, presence in each, "Christ within"

Z Personal inner-knowing light communication, "Holy Ghost"

ANCIENT PAST SIGN RULERS

"and, there shall be signs in the sun and moon and stars" gospel according to St. Luke XXI25

At a time when astrologers were only aware of seven planets, five were each given rulership of two signs. Those five were Mercury, Venus, Mars, Jupiter, and Saturn. The Sun and Moon were symbolically treated as planets and each was given one. The sign and planet rulers fell in a known, at the time, heavenly order.

Ruling Planet	Signs Ruled	
Mercury	Gemini	Virgo
Venus	Taurus	Libra
Mars	Aries	Scorpio
Jupiter	Pisces	Sagittarius
Saturn	Aquarius	Capricorn
Sun	Leo	
Moon	Cancer	

MODERN SIGN RULERS ADDED

As **Uranus** and **Neptune** were discovered, their rulership fell in placement and order in harmony with the original seven.

Saturn was then dropped as a ruler of Aquarius and that rulership assigned to the new planet Uranus. Jupiter's rulership of Pisces was in turn relinquished to newly discovered Neptune; this left only three planets: Mars, Venus, and Mercury, with dual rulerships. Planets discovered since the eighteenth century have brought great change and new awareness to mankind. At the time of the discovery of Uranus in 1781, Europe was in a great industrial revolution. Neptune, in 1846, influenced the introduction of anesthetics and gas lighting, bringing much emphasis on idealism and spiritualism in many new forms and expressions, as investigations through séances.

The new known planets Uranus and Neptune continued a rulership order to the signs Aquarius and Pisces in the Eleventh and Twelfth Houses. Saturn in the Eleventh and Jupiter in the Twelfth remain as Co-Rulers of those Signs and Houses.

Pluto's upheaval and breakthrough impact, added to the awakening influences of Neptune and Uranus, which brought dramatic public awareness and realizations of previously unheard of discoveries and inventions. Radio, telegraph, phonograph, telephone, aircraft and television, all unbelievable manifestations just a century earlier, became a very acceptable reality.

With the discovery of Pluto in 1930, by general consensus of astrologers, Mars was dropped as the ruler of Scorpio and given to Pluto, leaving the planet lineup "out of order." If, Pluto had been put in order in its heavenly position as the planet beyond Neptune, it would have been assigned as ruler of Aries, leaving Mars to hold its orderly position with Scorpio "Order is Heaven's first law." Pope

Pluto out of Order

Pluto in Order

NEW AGE RULING INFLUENCES

Today in the new Aquarian Age, a period when man has physically stepped on the Moon and is at work conquering space and bringing in tremendous changes in computer and satellite communications, we are again brought to an upheaval, a rearranging of old visions for new. We are directed to new insights for humanity relationships. There are new understandings of one's personal role and responsibility; change in direction of one's connection to the universe; a personal awareness of one's connection to the All. The new influence is present.

To date, no new planets have been recognized as "discovered." Although "undiscovered," this author believes there to be very definite separate vibrational influences to the signs Taurus and Gemini; influences which are similar to original assignment rulership or co-rulers—Venus with Taurus, and Mercury with Gemini. The *vibration* energy influence ruling Taurus, and represented in this book by "Symbol **X**," is similar in expression to its co-ruler Venus; however, the influence is of a very personal "inner-love" nature.

The *vibration* energy influence to Gemini is very similar to Mercury, its' co-ruler, but is a very personal "inner-light" quickening, an intuitive connection, represented in this book by "Symbol **Z**," of Omega, the end of a birth point, and moves through the houses and signs of experience. The cycle will end in the first astrological quarter of self and with Gemini, the personal inner communication third house and sign.

I do not know if the influence vibrations of "X" and/or "Z" are positioned farther out in space than Pluto, nor do I know if perhaps they are so close to earth and vibrating at such rapid speed that neither can presently be seen. The energy, though powerful, may not be physical, but that very personal "closer than hands and feet" connection to one's personal guiding, loving Presence.

As the New Age dawns, one becomes aware, more personally aware, of his/her Source connecting relationship. One begins to know and feel, the strong new "X" and "Z" influence; channeling a personal quickening energy of completion; and, at last will realize his/her oneness with Omnipotent Will, Omniscient Light, and Omnipresent Love.

PLANETARY RULERS AND CO-RULERS

While the Earth "appears" to spin in the heavens in one direction East to West, it actually rotates from West to East. All in the universe has a duality in direction: a Yin-Yang, positive-negative balance. An astrology chart can be read beginning from the eastern ascendant position through the 1st House, personal level, and continue on around through Houses 2 to 12 or, a reading may start from the Nadir, "beginning-end," foundation point of life, up through 7th-10th-1st Houses of experiences back to 4th Nadir. An "earth-time" concept reading would also begin at the Nadir (astrological midnight-new-day position), "IC-4th," reversing up through the 1st house ascendant, (daylight position) continuing through the 10th House (high-noon), mid-heaven down-through the descendent (dusk), and back through to the 4th house (midnight base).

The planet rulers also fall in Alternating directions while each ruler maintaining its exact heavenly order. The co-rulerships line-up is also in an exact order and identity with the signs of their original rulerships of ancient and past teachings.

There is a continuing order and connection of Rulers with Co-Rulers:

Rulers and Co-Rulers in Order

	RULING	CO-RULING
Z	Gemini	Virgo
X	Taurus	Libra
Pluto	Aries	Scorpio
Neptune	Pisces	Jupiter
Uranus	Aquarius	Saturn
Saturn	Capricorn	Aquarius
Jupiter	Sagittarius	Pisces
Mars	Scorpio	Aries
Venus	Libra	Taurus
Mercury	Virgo	Gemini
Sun	Leo	Cancer
Moon	Cancer	Leo

PLANETARY RULERS—CO RULERS

EXALTATION RULERS

What If our purpose-life goal, would be to express the best that we can be? After experiencing one's chart-life lessons through the many levels and possibilities of a sign, it's rulerships and aspect placements . . . What If our incarnation purpose would be "with eyes that could see:," to know and aspire to the best and highest level of expression with each sign and sign placement of position and aspect.? What If a level of perfection to do good, express good, and be good to "be ye therefore perfect as your father in heaven" were an aspiring goal? Can one achieve that level of growth? It must be possible or a master teacher (applicable in most religions) would not have directed us to do so What if the best, the perfection of one's incarnate goals could be known by what astrologers call exaltation rulerships?

Astrological Exaltation—a means of individual insight and growth; a high goal intent, positive, perfecting expression of life to discover and consciously fulfill. (Exaltations are explained at length in the individual sign chapters.)

There has been such confusion on the assignment of Planet Exaltations to signs, that the assignments are nearly as varied as the astrologers working with them. To this author's knowledge, very little work has been done to date with Astrological Exaltations by interpretation or application. Astrologers generally agree on the exaltation ruler assignments of <u>some</u> planets to zodiac signs. Many generally agree with the Suns exaltation in Aries and the Moon in Taurus. However, among astrologers there is still much individual difference of opinion and speculation of the exalted planet ruler-sign combinations.

In meditative query I asked, "why so much disagreement? What is the answer?" The "knowing inner-voice" response was clear. <u>"Order is the Law of the Universe."</u> Of course! All planets, signs, rulers fall in order! Eureka! So simple but where will this lead? What relationships will be made known? Place the houses, planets, signs in order and see. See a whole new (old?) exciting, deductive revelation of planet/sign relationships slowly unfolding in continuous order and meaningful application. The exaltation placement of planets to signs is in the <u>same exact</u> order as is present with all rulership position placements.

RULERS—CO-RULERS—EXALTATION RULERS

There is a working harmonious relationship among all planets and their signs. The Universe must be—every part—in perfect order, DIVINE ORDER IS THE LAW OF THE UNIVERSE. "The law of the Lord is perfect:" Psalms: 19:7

"I know this world is ruled by infinite intelligence. It required infinite intelligence to create it, and it requires infinite intelligence to keep it on its course. Everything that surrounds us—everything that exists—proves that there are infinite laws behind it. There can be no denying this fact. It is mathematical in its precision." Thomas Alva Edison.

THE PLANETS APPLIED

SUN
Ego Identity, Essential Self, Character Potential, Vital Power Source, Purpose
Rules **Leo**—heart creative center, love Spirit
Co-Rules **Cancer**—unites ego with nurturing foundation (mother /father source)
Exaltation **Aries**—spirit WILL, personal goal identity "I AM"

MOON
Personality, Sun Reflection, Psyche, Soul, Subconscious, Instincts, Habits,
Rules **Cancer**—Will base, reactive emotion, instincts, habits, memory
Co-Rules **Leo**—reflects emotional strength and power.
Exaltation **Taurus**—LOVE reflected through personality manifestations.

MERCURY
Communicating, Coordinating Expressions, Reasoning, Intellect, Mind
Rules **Virgo**—intelligence to analytical, investigative, discerning communication
Co-Rules **Z**—connects outer reasoning communication to inner knowing
Exaltation **Pisces**—emotional LIGHT insight of vision and wisdom

VENUS
Sensory Feeling Relationships, Harmony, Beauty, Arts, Love
Rules **Libra**—fosters harmony and balance in relationships, partnerships
with others
Co-Rules **Taurus**—awakens to senses of love and beauty presence
Exaltation **Aquarius**—develops humanity unity and harmony—Agape LOVE

MARS
Initiates Action, Directed Energy Demonstration, Assertive Action, Desire
Rules **Scorpio**—securing sexual love partnerships, generational security
Co-Rules **Aries**—initial "me first" self motivated survival energy force
Exaltation **Capricorn**—aspiring WILL goals of energy, directed public action

JUPITER
Growth and Expansion of Consciousness, Abundance, Luck, Beneficial, Ethics
Rules **Sagittarius**—truth search expansion through knowledge, philosophy, travel
Co-Rules **Pisces**—expanding vision through optimistic beliefs, faith, and charity
Exaltation **Sagittarius**—transcending consciousness expansion to Spirit LIGHT

SATURN
Responsible Character Building, Duty, Restriction, Structure, Karma
Rules **Capricorn**—self discipline-sacrifice to perfect and refine individual will
Co-Rules **Aquarius**—serving mankind, responsibility to society
Exaltation **Scorpio**—ego sacrifice, loyalty LOVE of another, emotional refinement

URANUS   Awareness, Freedom, Change, Upheaval, Revolution, Futuristic, Eccentric.
Rules **Aquarius**—awareness perception of self in relation to others
Co-Rules **Capricorn**—awareness evaluation (judgment) of one's growth progress
Exaltation **Libra**—aware of the individual WILL of another, balance through unity

NEPTUNE   Social Vision, Understanding Wisdom, Imagination, Dreams, Idealistic
Rules **Pisces**—intuitive sensitivity, emotional depth, humility in wisdom
Co-Rules **Sagittarius**—idealistic truth optimism, enthusiastic social vision
Exaltation **Virgo**—wisdom LIGHT with purity of intent, altruistic service to others

PLUTO   Elimination, Regeneration, Resurrection, Transformation, Death-Rebirth
Rules **Aries**—personal life resurrection regenerating from ego ashes
Co-Rules **Scorpio**—renewal through life-death cycles
Exaltation **Leo**—new Spirit creation birth from the hearts LOVE Center Source

X   Very Personal Vibrating, Motivating Presence, "Christ Within" in each
Rules **Taurus**—love presence within evokes personal security
Co-Rules **Libra**—presence within balances ability to relate to another in love
Exaltation **Cancer**—"Christ Within" WILL stimulus to a nurturing caring soul

Z   Very Personal Inner "Knowing Light" (Holy Ghost) Communication
Rules **Gemini**—impressions of psychic, telepathy, clairvoyance, etc. phenomenon
Co-Rules **Virgo**—inner light discernment
Exaltation **Gemini**—one's guiding LIGHT "holy ghost" inner voice knowing

DETRIMENT AND FALL COMMENTS

It is this author's belief that there are no detriment or fall rulerships that all planet energies are for good. If there be a detriment or fall expression, that expression is a result of individual choice action.

"The problem, Dear Brutus, is not in our stars, but in ourselves" Shakespeare.

There is a Law-omnipotent force, at work in and through man, and the Universe. This same Law that directs our solar system directs all of life to individual perfection. The transiting planet stimulates an action and a life experience comes. Each individual responds from an "inner-directed" or an "outer-reactive" position. Aware or unaware, a creative choice, "free will" is made within one's fixed design, (which is represented by an astrology chart or life map.) The free will concept brings to mind some wise words from a wonderful old song, "You gotta accentuate the positive, eliminate the negative, latch on to the affirmative." Each choice brings its specific results. The great Law of Cause and Effect is in operation. Results of choices teach life's lessons, and so one grows.

There are no "bad" astrology charts. It is this author's belief that each individual soul progresses through many experiences in many lifetimes, and that in each lifetime incarnates to the situation (i.e., family and cultural environment) needed for continuous soul growth until one evolves from the law of rebirth. Each re-embodiment gives new opportunities of experience to fulfill one's individual destiny to wholeness-holiness.

An astrology chart/map shows the present life's specific preplanned guide, needed experience schedule; a map showing a part of the whole plan for each one toward his/her continuous growth to perfection. The soul progresses through many experiences of learning Light and experiencing Love, for self-mastery to perfection. We are each a part of others, and the Spirit is within each. One's physical existence is for personal growth, and to be a part of the growth process of others. Each Life Is Meant for Good.

ABOUT ASTROLOGICAL ASPECTS

Aspects symbolize energies in our life meant for personal growth and fulfillment.

Aspects define and focus (delineate) the types of experience-relationships which will evolve within the self and with others in the many areas of our lives. There are no "bad" aspects. The misapplication of experience brings pain. The same aspect can disable an unaware individual, or be the goad for tremendous success to an enlightened soul.

Trying experiences teach lessons which could come in no other way. For example, square 90 degree aspects may bring obstacles and challenges, which might be viewed as a motivator to build one's character through the constructive action of overcoming. Through strife and conflict, one comes into contact with the inner strength of divine Self and achieves conquest to greater heights. Squares are stepping stones to spiritual achievement.

> "Difficulties show men what they are. In case of any difficulty, God has pitted you against a rough antagonist that you may be a conqueror, and this cannot be without toil." Epictetus

The opposition 180 degrees may trigger awareness, teaching individual reflection through conflicting balance awareness of another individual or situation. Energy often cannot be known or understood without its opposing energy to show balance. One can recognize truth through having experienced error. The choice of action is within the individual. For example, planets in opposition in the 2nd and 8th houses (security, love houses) indicate that when one is in harmony with, and can love self (2nd house,) then one is capable of projecting that love to another (8th house.) "When I love me—I am able to love thee."

Aspects that are traditionally labeled good can be just as challenging. A conjunction (0 degrees) brings concentrated power to an area where harmony lessons must be learned. A trine, (120 degrees) can be so easy that one must be alert not to be complacent or lazy, but to use this aspect as a great opportunity for cooperation and harmony achievements.

Our actions-reactions to aspects; indeed, to life, are as truly individual as the one experiencing. The astrological chart shows the potentials existent within an individual life, and time periods shown by transit and progression, when these potentials are likely to manifest. Hypothetically, two individuals born at the same moment and space in time would have nearly identical experiences during their lifetimes; but will not act upon those experiences in the same manner. The result and quality of life will be different. Each one has an individuality to fulfill!

COMBINING PARTS—
FULFILLING SIGNS

COMBINING PARTS—FULFILLING SIGNS

"It is only by the vision of wisdom that the horoscope of the ages can be read"
Emerson

The reading of an astrological chart generally involves the interpretive application of the planetary body rulers and co-rulers to the individual signs and houses in relationship to each and the whole. An astrological reading can give a good functional understanding (depending on the ability of the reader) of an individual, an individual's relationships, or insight to any unlimited number of situations and/or experiences. As one understands the "whys" of self and surroundings through astrology, one of the many tools of interpretive understanding, one begins to improve his/her quality of life. Then comes the bigger questions that each one is directed to ponder and openly question at sometime in his/her growth evolvement in life, the "whys of purpose." "Why am I here?" "What specific goals am I to fulfill?" An exaltation ruler to an individual chart can direct one to move toward one's personal goal expressions as seen in the individual's astrology chart, life map.

As you read through the following sign chapters, please remember that each sign is expressed somewhere in each individual chart, to mentally apply insights of application.

Each signs chapter will briefly describe the connection of the planetary body Ruler, Co-Ruler, and Exaltation Ruler of the sign, house, and symbols in interpretive relationships. The emphasis of interpretation will be on the planetary body Exaltation Ruler to its sign and symbols. Through the exaltation understanding, we can realize the goal expression of the sign and it's potential fulfillment possibilities by individual placement and application; an application of self knowledge to joyful understanding wisdom!

CANCER

Quality	Cardinal Will
Element	Water Emotional
Symbol	Crab
House	Fourth-Nadir
Ruler	**Moon** . . . personality, psyche-soul, mother, changing, memory, habitual life
Co-Ruler	**Sun** . . . will source foundation, father
Exaltation Ruler	**"X"** . . . divine emotional inner soul activating Source.
X glyph	The cross X . . . symbolizes crossing out, eliminating human personality from the total self, crucifying the human personality for the divine life that cannot be destroyed.
	The cross in exalted position X symbolizes the four bodies of man (physical, emotional, mental and spiritual) in perfect balance united in one soul joining in a focus centered in ones personal identity to his divine Source

"The decussated cross implies that the central point is not limited to one individual however perfect. That the Principle (God) is in humanity and humanity, as all the rest, is in it, like drops of water are in the ocean, the four ends being toward the four cardinal points, hence loosing themselves in infinity.". *The Secret Doctrine.* Blavatsky.

x glyph

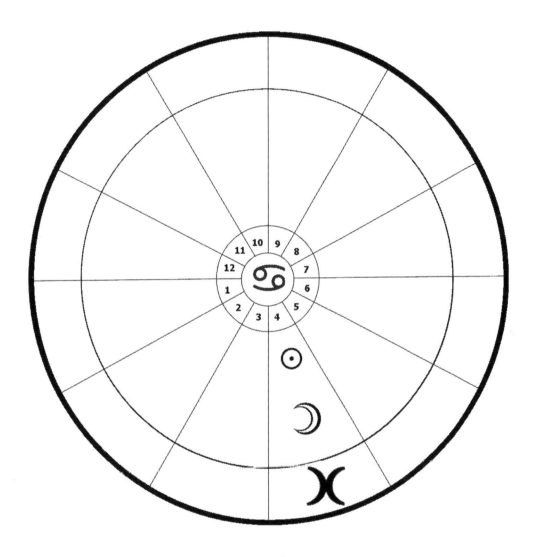

cancer chart

CANCER

An astrological sign is best defined through the meaning of its many symbols. Cancer, a cardinal-water sign, exemplifies the trait of emotional (water) will (cardinal); the will to emotionally express caring feelings. This quality potential is present wherever, and to the degree, the sign is found in one's map-plan, as can be seen in an astrology chart

The Moon, Cancer's astrological ruler, represents the soul-psyche; the emotional subconscious base of the personality of the self. Cancer's co-ruler the Sun, represents personal will. The Moon reflects the Sun. The psyche-soul personality (Moon) of self-reflects the personal will (Sun) of self. The Moon, ruler of Cancer and a mother symbol, unites with the Sun, co-ruler and father symbol—a united creative father-mother base or source of life.

The fourth house of Cancer astrologically represents the base foundation, or Nadir position; the home or house in which one lives. Cancer's fourth house placement then tells us that the sign is an expression of where one feels strong roots. The individual placement may be in any area of life, depending on Cancer's position in the individual's chart. The house of mans being is his body, or the whole of his bodies, including the physical, emotional, mental and spiritual bodies of self. The representative symbol of the sign Cancer is the crab, one that carries its home with him. The crab moves backward, sideways and forward, assimilating from all circumferences within its reach, representing one who tenaciously holds on to thoughts and memories of the past, while assimilating from present and on-going experiences. The symbolic connection of the past and future is as real for Cancer as that of the present. The exterior shell of the crab is as the personality shell of man. The crab cannot grow while it is enclosed in its shell, it must molt the old shell, and then the inner body grows larger by taking in large quantities of water. After inner growth, a new and larger shell is grown to accommodate the expanded body. Man, as the crab, will also shed his "hard outer shell" mask of personality, by the conscious use (will) of large quantities of caring emotion, symbolized by water. One must be vulnerable for a time, drop his/her protective shell and show caring, nurturing emotion; thus expand the inner soul body. When this is done, a new, broader emotionally expanded personality emerges. New life begins from the inner soul level, the womb of the self, from that resting place before physical manifestation symbolized astrologically by the nadir-midnight which proceeds the new day. In time, the expanded soul awakens to a higher level of being within body manifestation; it identifies with its Divine Love-emotion mother (moon ruler) and Divine Will father (Sun co-ruler) Source, developing an awareness of the true Source, foundation of one's being. The merging personality of the soul united with the divine inner-core spark produces new life, the "holy-whole" child "X" is born.

"X" is the exaltation symbol of the sign Cancer, representing the very personal inner love nature present within each soul waiting to be released, to be born into man—manifestation. The personal inner love nature "X" evolves from the Soul, that foundation home base of man which has existed from the beginning; the Soul-psyche that original Self sent forth from the Omnipresent Spirit as a pure living essence, recording impressions, developing traits and habits, forming character from individualizing self experiences. Each soul is free to build his/her own house of experiences through, and from one's choice of actions; developing habits, fears, likes, dislikes—all forming character trait recordings as tapes in the memory bank of the soul. The exaltation influence of the sign Cancer symbolizes the goal of each transcending one to release, unfold, the un-manifested divine potential of the self. Living experience brings growth to perfection. This may take many lives, many personality "shell sheddings." One lifetime, however long, would not reasonably produce the vast number of experiences necessary to know and exhibit ones wholeness-holiness! "Perfection is attained by slow degrees; it requires the hand of time." Voltaire

Might it not be reasonable to believe that for continuing inner growth, one must periodically shed the outer physical shell; literally shed the physical body so that from the soul of self one may objectively observe the physical life just completed and, with guidance from one's omnipotent presence, evaluate lessons learned and lessons that are still to be worked through. It would seem that from the clear vantage point, away and apart from physical personality and physical body that the soul could see the past, present, and future of the self and might choose or be guided to a new place and a new set of circumstances or boundaries, as seen in a zodiac map. For each individual to experience, and to reap the harvest of lessons learned, to have an opportunity to sow new seed, learn new lessons still needed for growth, a new incarnation—a fresh start, would give an opportunity to make right, past errors of experience. In time—lifetimes, one might evolve to a place where he or she will "go out no more;" will no longer necessarily be bound to a karmic map. In time a growing awareness of the divine Source within, becomes one's own personal savior from the continuous cycle of karmic law incarnations The soul fully centered in divine Source is free from human consciousness, from ego personality-identity and has overcome sins (errors of ignorance) from the past; has overcome the outer physical world body, and then functions from the indwelling Source.

"The soul of man is like to water, from Heaven it cometh to Heaven it riseth and then returneth to earth, forever alternating." J.W. Goethe

"Every soul is immortal for whatever is in perpetual motion is immortal. All that is soul presides over all that is without soul and patrols all heaven, now appearing in one form and now in another . . . every man's soul has by the law of his birth been a spectator of eternal truth, or it never would have passed into this our mortal frame, yet still it is no easy matter for all to be a reminder of their past by their present existence." Plato.

LEO

Quality	Fixed Love
Element	Fire Spirit
Symbol	Lion
House	Fifth
Ruler	**Sun** . . . ego, creation, heart energy center, father, Spirit
Co Ruler	**Moon** . . . personality, soul reflection, love, mother base
Exaltation Ruler	**Pluto** . . . planet of rebirth, regeneration, spirit resurrection
Pluto Glyph	represents the triumph of Spirit over the receptive personality, and over the physical natural body.

pluto glyph

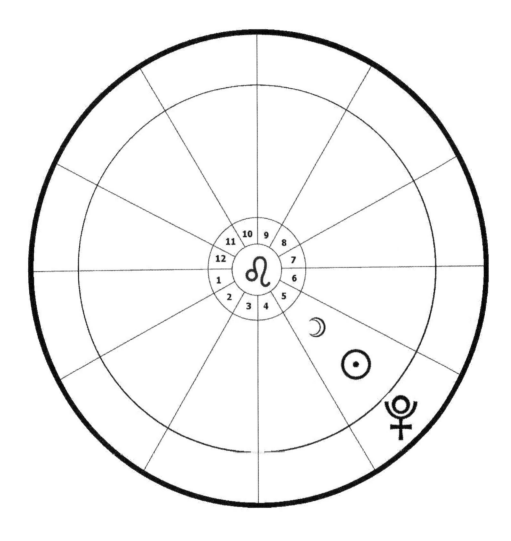

leo chart

LEO

Leo, the fire, fixed-security sign signifies the expression of spirit love. Leo, exemplifying spirit love, rules the heart which is the love life center of man. The focus of love in each one is from the heart. The Sun is the heart center of all life—the divine, heart-source energy of man's being. Spirit, is astrologically represented by the Sun, planetary-body ruler of Leo.

The Moon, Leo's co-ruler, represents the feminine receptive personality in each one. As the Moon reflects the Sun, so also does the astrological moon (personality symbol) reflect the Sun (astrological heart Spirit—ego center) from whatever level the Sun is projecting. The uniting of Sun, father symbol (Leo ruler) and reflecting mother symbol Moon (Leo co-ruler,) represent the unity of soul and spirit to give birth, to project or create the child. "I create what I Am." The I AM Source, living essence of man, is the creative life—the father-mother principal of life. Love is the creative power of the universe.

Leo is placed in the fifth house of creation and love. In this house of one-to-one love relationships, one seeks love expression in and through love affairs in a search to fulfill and find the self worthy of love; one learns of love in identity security relationships. Projecting the self into the world through the biological love creating of children, secures ones continuing identity. Creative love is also expressed through the arts as love sent forth and solidified through the many avenues of artistic creative production and/or demonstration, as in painting, writing, dancing, singing and dramatic acting. Each one identifies with his creation. Where the sign Leo is found in an individual chart, denotes an area, place or opportunity for growth in love through creative expression.

The fifth house of Leo also symbolically represents the teacher of children. Each one in time, grows to learn through an open reception, as children, to the teaching voice of the high Self from within. There can be no other true teacher, but the Source of ones being teaching from the heart. The quiet, inner place in ones heart is the place of divine inspiration, and each one, alone, must find that place. When one arrives at the level where he/she no longer seeks nor accepts the repeated words of confusion, echoed from the mouths of others, one becomes king of his/her being, ruling from the teachings of the kingdom within—from the divine Source. Just as the Lion, king of beasts and symbol of the sign Leo, has dominion of the animal world, so also has each individual dominion of his/her physical world. One is king and ruler of his/her animal self whose conscious goal is to seek guidance from the divine Source center of the heart. Each and every one has a natural physical body and an inherent spiritual body. When one truly becomes aware of his/her divine spiritual connection, the only life Source, he/she is raised to a new birth, reborn, aware and functioning from Spirit. Love opens the life force, the created energy expressing to make one aware of his/her connection to the omnipresent life Source.

Pluto, the planet exalted in the sign of Leo, represents the triumph of spirit over the receptive personality and over the physical natural body (see glyph interpretation). Pluto was named after the god of Hades to indicate a resurrection from the ashes or fires of

Hell. The ashes of Hell are symbolic of the memories and pains of trial and error physical body experiences made pure through experience fires. Divine Spirit (fire) emits the spark of human spirit to symbolically burn, purify and renew the soul. The fire of Spirit is the purifying agent. Pluto's erratic, compulsive force brings one's life to upheaval, forcing one to see the naked facts of error in an area or experience of life. This is necessary before one can give birth-re-birth to the child within, the rebirth of spirit to the pain, contractions and physical upheaval in the labor experience preceding childbirth. The human identity consciousness must give way to its spirit identity. All are children of the one divine Source. Man must refine the self, let go of the old; transform the ego-child to new creation, a new birth awareness child of the divine creator, father-mother Source.

"Your children are not your children, they are the sons and daughters of life's longing for itself. They came through you, but not from you. You are the bows from which your children as living arrows are sent forth." *The Prophet*—Kahlil Gibran.

VIRGO

Quality	Mutable-Light
Element	Earth-Physical
Symbol	Virgin
House	Sixth
Ruler	**Mercury** communicating intellect with discriminating purity of thought.
Co-Ruler	**"Z"** communicating intuitively, inner-knowing connection.
Exaltation Ruler	**Neptune** physically demonstrating light-wisdom through understanding service to wisdom in action.
Neptune Glyph	The Neptune glyph is the physical cross rising into personality expression, resulting in trinity exalted over matter. The physical symbolically merges with the other three parts of self (emotional, mental and spiritual)l to merge into the divine whole or unity of self expressing in outer personality manifestation.

neptune glyph

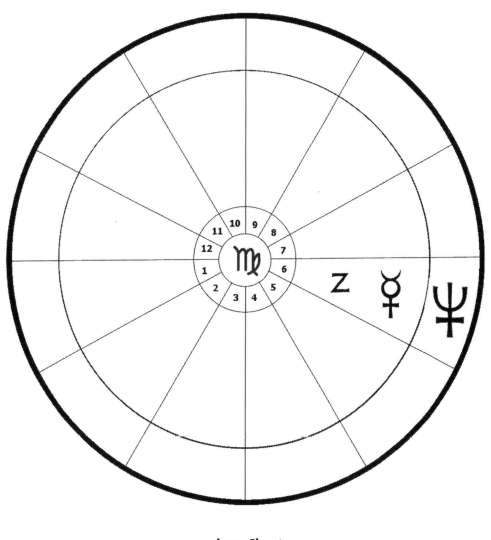

virgo Chart

VIRGO

Virgo, sign of the Virgin, is a feminine receptive sign. Virgo's symbol is composed of the ancient letter M meaning water, psyche or soul; and in Hebrew, M spelled mem, means mother. The attached glyph (see chart) means fish and in Latin is interpreted a higher power. The Omnipotent life power within each human life in time, stimulates in each one, evolvement to purity of soul. It is the destiny of the pure Virgin soul to give life to its divinity. Virgo, mutable earth sign represents man's physical demonstration (earth,) a bringing forth of the inner-light (mutable) into visible manifestation. Man is a seed from the blueprint of perfection, a pure source, with inherent potential, capable of blossoming into outer divine growth.

Mercury, communication planet and ruler of the sign Virgo, assists in directing intelligence to produce the manifestation of light. Mercury's energy must be used in clear, unbiased thinking, with an open mind to learn. The function of the mind is to question, investigate and learn. "It is good to be a seeker, but sooner or later you have to be a finder." Jonathan Livingston Seagull. Truth enlightenment comes through application of the Virgo qualities of analytical study, assimilation and organization of facts, from considered judgment, reasoning, and practical growth experience.

The personal intuitive discernment and knowing inner-guide assistance, as represented by "Z", co-ruling influence, is given as one becomes aware in light to consciously practice truth and purity of thought. Pure thought physically expressed invokes the true power of becoming. One possesses, becomes a part of, the words and deeds he/she expresses. To harvest or manifest the "good fruits" of life, of personal well-being, one must sow the "good seeds" of thought and service to all.

Virgo's natural home base is in the sixth and final house below the horizon; the house of health, service and personal harvest. Every seed produces after its kind, the nature of effect is always in accordance with the nature of cause. Man must harvest and separate good nourishing seed of thoughts from worthless error-thought seed. Thoughts truly are things. The thoughts and words of ones conviction become the realities of ones life "They can because they think they can." Virgil.

Good health is an outward expression of harmony within. There is a divine healing-presence, inner-life energy always at work, renewing and making whole. It is man's faith (focus of attention) that determines his well-being. Each one receives exactly what he expects to receive. If one focuses on thoughts of poor health claims, sickness and disease, those thoughts will produce in kind. Thoughts of fear, anxiety, anger, etc., will hinder and block the body's natural flow. Immediate observation of this is in seeing ones nervous blush, the manifestation of one "frozen" in fear, or in observing the fainting of one who has just heard traumatic shocking news. Thoughts and words have tremendous impact on the physical body. Is ones belief-faith (focus of attention) on sickness or health—to manifest illness or wholeness? Each has dominion of his/her thoughts, one's focus of attention and beliefs are sent forth into manifestation from the impartial, renewing, life-force power within; in light and truth, one can be restored to health.

Thoughts centered on ones divine energy Source are also made applicable in fulfilling and practical works, through service to others. Each man must live according to his own light, his own understanding. "Man's greatness lies in his power of thought." Pascal.

Neptune, the planet symbolizing discerning wisdom and understanding, is exalted in the sign Virgo. Wherever Virgo or Neptune is found in one's chart may indicate a high goal exaltation interpretation, a place where one has the opportunity to express and know oneness in light—know unity of self; to loose the ego-self to life's guiding Source and use the physical body as an instrument of service to others. Neptune's influence, if not individually expressed in full light awareness, might indicate an area in life's pattern of confusion or illusion. The Neptune goal is to personally live the dream, the ideal to 'Be,' to manifest the vision, the physical insight light. In its most idealistic state, Virgo would be working in pure (virgin) divine light of discriminating wisdom, with insight to commit an act because it is essential and right. Work influenced by the opinions or rewards of another is illusion and less than true to the self. Each must live according to his/her own understanding and to allow another, without criticism, to do the same. We criticize what we don't understand. If another walks a different path, know there are many avenues of experience to the same Source, none ever exactly the same, and some very different. If another appears to walk in darkness, see that one in light, as a young student reaping and sowing, struggling in the school of life. Understand, forgive, think well of each, and respond in kindness. This sends a helpful vibration and so assists each one, in a step forward to higher light expression. Teaching or learning must fall on outer man before it can awaken inner-man. Inner knowledge, higher understanding, comes only when one is ready in purity of thought as words may be pious and detrimental. Each one is the teacher of another by understanding and by example.

The Virgo exaltation goal is to manifest pure substance of being "be ye therefore perfect". With purity of intent, each one must work—strive to live the ideal, to transform the self through service and example to others; and, in the law of consequences, what is given will be reaped in bountiful harvest, As one sees truth in another, one finds self-knowledge. From new summits of experience, one can know new peaks of understanding.

"All that man can possibly do, be, or become, is now within him, an undeveloped possibility of attainment. It is for him to bring forth and, in the light of a knowledge and understanding of Truth. Lift it to the plane where it belongs." Fayette M. Drake

LIBRA

Quality	Cardinal Will
Element	Air Mental
Symbol	Scales (balance)
House	Seventh
Ruler	**Venus** sensitivity to harmony and beauty learned through balancing relationships
Co-Ruler	**"X"** personal harmony identity. Inner-love—presence necessary for outer harmony relationships.
Exaltation Ruler	**Uranus** awareness of unity connection of self and another balancing and fulfilling each.
Uranus Glyph	The Uranus glyph is composed of the physical cross resting on a spirit foundation, working through opposing physical earth expressions as masculine-feminine, from the balanced position of two opposing personalities; facing East representing the ascendant-self personality and facing West representing the descendent—other personality. The cross of physical contrast unites and balances opposing personalities and expressions of opposition from an operating spirit base. Uranus symbolizes a unity awareness of one to another—others.

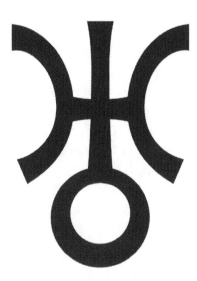

uranus glyph

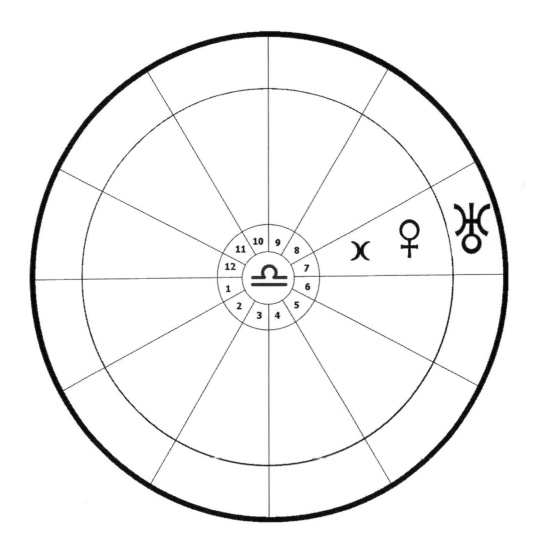

libra chart

LIBRA

Libra, the cardinal air sign demonstrates the combined quality of will (cardinal) and air (mental), or the uniting of the ego self to another through conscious mental application. Libra the sign of partnerships, is the beginning sign on the descendent where one leaves self and unites with another to begin the ascent of identity through others from "me to thee." Libra, symbolized by the scales of balance, teaches through life's many balances as positive-negative, masculine feminine, east-west, and is at home in the seventh house of marriage and partnerships. In this house, one finds balance of self through another; one can know and see the self through another. Through personal one-to-one relationships, each chooses a partner from the opposition point; from ascendant (first house) of self image, to the opposition descendant (seventh house) partner position, to reflect and balance the self. "Through my partner, my close friend, I see myself."

Venus, the planet of the senses and of feeling relationships is the planetary ruler of Libra. The Venus influence instigates harmony lessons through the love-feeling partner relationships, blending and transferring those feelings from self to another. Positive caring feelings balanced for and with another contribute to a relationship of blessings, one of harmony and peace. Libra teaches relationship lessons through experiences of opposites and opposition. So, while the Venus influence can bring qualities of love and beauty to a relationship, there is also the potential of hate and ugliness. The negative expressions are, in astrological vocabulary, sometimes considered a "detriment." It is not the sign or planet that is in "detriment," but one's misuse or misapplication of universal energy. The potential of extremes in expression is symbolically present in every planet sign relationship. The lessons of the world are for many reasons; no part of any experience or relationship is without purpose or benefit. Each one attracts experiences to develop growth awareness. The response to a situation is the "spiritual report card," and much more important than the situation. In this vein, each encounter we meet brings good to our life as it brings another growth opportunity. How truly can any expression be labeled detrimental or bad if that experience of contrast is needed or useful to know balance? Can one know light without the experience of darkness? Is experience the key to really knowing? Might it not be the reason for our long journey of incarnations from and back to the Source of all life? All things work for good in Divine Law. One learns the lessons of balance as one evolves through the experiences of contrast: relationships. An Astrology chart will show where Libra is teaching balance in one's life.

The co-ruler influence of Libra is the personal love identity influence, "X," always present in each individual soul. To love—see the inner beauty "X" in another, one must love and see the inner beauty of self. To love is to understand, to call forth the love-energy of the self; to see love one must love. An aware one would strive to meet adversity or personal attack in a loving view. Every life, no matter how negatively expressed, has an inner meaning, a beautiful potential, and an inner glory. If one can see another's unkindness from a new perspective, "turn the other cheek," look again, and see from a new view, a new mental awareness from divine will, one can then consciously demonstrate love-action relationships at work in and through the self. A high inner-love "X" expression between aware ones is one of detachment and freedom, even and particularly, in the close relationship of marriage. A clinging, smothering, holding relationship is misdirected love evolving from an absence awareness of personal inner love. The one knowingly connected to his/her love Source relies on his/her inner love identity rather than the ambiguous reflection of another's approval. A true love-feeling relationship is to honestly be able to grow alone together, giving and accepting freely the nurturing, caring support of the partner.

> "Let there he spaces in your togetherness . . . Love one another, but make not a bond of love: Let it rather be a moving sea between the shores of your souls . . . give your hearts, but not into each others keeping. For only the hand of Life can contain your hearts." *The Prophet*, Kahlil Gibran.

Uranus, the exaltation planet ruler of Libra, evokes change in relationship awareness. Through mental will, conscious awareness application, one can uproot outlived stifling relationship attitudes to an awakening, evolving higher consciousness. This planet of freedom, change, and reform works to express transformation of purpose from freedom of ego-self to will, to evolve higher love awareness, a caring partner to each as one; to unite the self with the "All."

This is the mystical marriage: 1) to willfully unite the divine essence of self with the divine essence of another, knowing they are, and have always been the same—knowing that the only true life is One omnipresent life; and, 2) to consciously unite the individual human-ego will with the divine Will Source of its being. This union, this marriage, is the "'holy-whole" bond that cannot be divided. Man cannot be separated from his omnipresent, omnipotent Source. The choice to use that one power for "good" or "evil" is within each one. The power "to do;" the life force of man and all things is of the One universal Source. The "for" or "against" is man's choice, and the law of cause and effect is divine power-Will, in action. The logical process by which divine power manifests the Law, is always working; aware or unaware, man demonstrates the law.

Libra, sign of law, teaches us to work with the Law in aware, conscious realization. The knowing man can unfold his destiny, discover the living essence from within, and evolve from his Source.

To awaken to the discovery of ones unity-connection of self to each, in and through the one Source; and to consciously mentally function in and from ones divine Will relationship, is the Libra exaltation goal. Through this goal one will find an open door to the wonderful fruits of love, joy, peace, beauty and many other fulfilling expressions, waiting to be discovered, developed and released. To this end-goal, one will attain divine growth and the blessings therein.

> "Finally Brethren, whatsoever things are true, whatsoever things are honest, whatsoever things are just, whatsoever things are pure, whatsoever things are lovely, whatsoever things are of good report; if there be any virtue, and if there be any praise think on these things." Philippians-epistle of Paul

SCORPIO

Quality	Fixed Love
Element	Water Emotional
Symbols	Scorpion, Serpent, Eagle, Phoenix Bird
House	Eighth
Ruler	**Mars** . . . love energy (sexual) expression, securing emotional marriage relationship.
Co-Ruler	**Pluto** . . . renewal of emotional love nature, regeneration evolution
Exaltation Ruler	**Saturn** . . . harvest, reaping, life/death mysteries, personality sacrifice, responsible life perfecting love transformation.
Saturn Glyph	The Cross . . . physical symbol of over coming good-evil human consciousness, is lifted over personality as a resurrected symbol of the divine power within man, overcoming and ruling physical man-ego personality.

saturn glyph

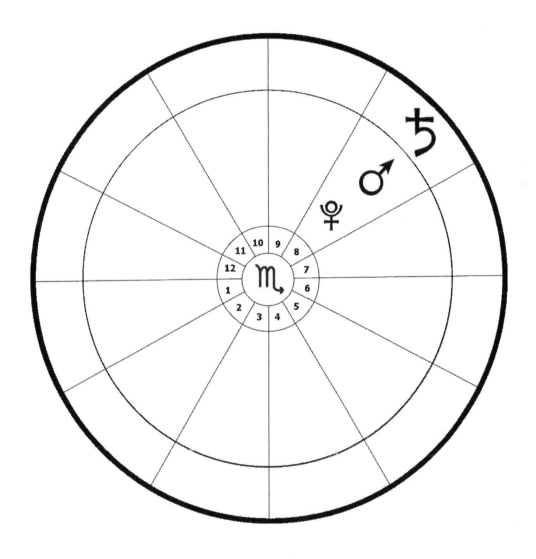

scorpio chart

SCORPIO

The Scorpio glyph is of the ancient letter "M" Water symbol, astrologically representing intuitive emotional sensitivity, deep dimensions of the inner self and feelings, projected and directed by the cross(ancient symbol of matter) of earth experiences into an outer productive consciousness. Scorpio, quality of fixed security with the element water, which projects the emotional (water) love (fixed-security) characteristic of expression. Scorpio represents emotional regeneration of life-giving energy.

The sign reigns in the eighth house of love secured through a one-to-one partnership as in and through the security of a marriage relationship. Scorpio's element water, depicts the deep psychological emotional desire body and also represents the living water of life projected through vital sex fluids.

Mars, Scorpio's ruler, often labeled the sex planet, rules the sex fluids regulating life and death. Physical sex impregnates the life seed securing future generations and securing the marriage in an active deep emotional relationship. The Mars love energy is best expressed through the marriage relationship responsibly, securing the marriage partnership and the social security of mankind.

Pluto, co-ruler of Scorpio, is the planet interpretatively associated with life, resurrected life, and death (including Hades) and with the hidden mysteries of life and death. Pluto assists to transform the Scorpio emotional energy from a self-gratifying "hell level" of experience and expression to a renewed higher level. The inner-nature of man is continuously being renewed through the overcoming of trial-error experiences. The Pluto influence is at work to eliminate energy waste and destroy the useless; leaving the renewed inner-self free to be reborn from the death of the carnal love, self.

The several animal and mythological symbols of Scorpio represent stages of mankind's regenerative evolution. The Scorpion, small, ugly animal of the earth with its dangerous poisonous sting, and the low crawling Serpent. Both representing earthbound man moving, struggling on an emotional reactive stomach, responding at a low level, stinging, poisoning others to protect self, a misusing of the life energy of self.

The Eagle, another symbol, moves higher beyond self, loyal to partner by mating and staying with only one partner, to soar above the earth high and free. The Phoenix bird, a fabled bird in Greek mythology. is also a Scorpio symbol. The Phoenix, larger than the eagle is to have lived a very long life renewed from the ashes of self, symbolizing the immortal, spiritual rebirth potential of man. Each is symbolically striving; one will at some time in the soul's evolution, from the ashes of destructive experiences, realize his/her eternal life core and will consciously relinquish the personal perishable small ego self-identity. To live one must lose the self; die to the senses, to renewed—emotional regeneration, to find the true center-Source of self. "He that dies not before he dies will find he is dead after he dies." Jacob Boehme.

Saturn, the exalted planet ruler of the sign Scorpio, signifies the higher esoteric hidden meaning in this eighth house of deep mystery truths. Saturn is symbolized as the cross over the crescent Moon of personality. The Scorpio goal of each one is to sacrifice the human personality on the cross of physical matter and limitation to new resurrected life. The Scorpio symbol also has the cross directed up to signify emotional resurrected goals. On the long road to meet the exalted Scorpio level of being, man encounters and overcomes "good-evil" consciousness. Saturn can be symbolic of the "good"-Divine, or "evil"-Satan consciousness in man. Lucifer is light fallen from the heavens (high place of consciousness) allegorically representing the fall in any man who moves from the light of his divine Source consciousness. To know the divine source, man descends through earth contacts and experiences of contrast, before his/her ascension to high conscious awareness. The life Source is always present in all, even in the greatest darkness of the soul. Each one is at times confronted with a part of his/her own dark nature (human devil) and the hell of ones own making. Hell literally means to build a wall around, to be cut off from, as one in dark consciousness cuts the self off from, the indwelling Source. Hell might truly be a state of existence ready for purification. When the desire to no longer suffer from choices made in darkness (error) is strong, the divine desire spark of Spirit may light the fires of purification to burn the garbage (fear, anger, hate, etc.) within. The word hell, comes from the Aramaic word ghenna, a place where all the refuse of Jerusalem was cast. This fire continuously burned to destroy the discarded garbage to purifying one's living area.

Saturn, also ruler of karmic law and often labeled the grim reaper, disciplines, teaches, and perfects the soul through many experiences in sowing and reaping, cause and effect, darkness and light—all encounters through many lives of experience to return man to his divine Source. Each soul must struggle with his/her individual overcoming, good-evil extremes of self; each meets life's lessons in error, by resisting evil. Each one has the power from his/her omnipotent Source to cast out his human error emotions and actions; to end the misuse of creative force and return good for evil; a greater light for lesser light. As each one can banish, (remove temptation,) his/her human error consciousness (devil) is overcome by and through inner divine-Source guidance. To know physical death is but change to another level of experience, an entrance to a new opportunity of life, truly revealing an exalted awareness of Saturn's grim reaper transforming to life's divine reaper.

When one gives-up (sacrifices) the ego-desire error life of the past, he or she is renewed in and through a universal life force of love; emphasis is then on a transforming personal love energy projected beyond personality self, to loving another as self.

An increase and fulfilling of self is realized as one's love energy is sent out to another. Each one may realize the Scorpio exaltation goal when he/she understands and demonstrates the great Love Life-Spirit of One, present in each. This Spirit moving in manifestation is the continuous never-dying life force without beginning or end.

"Love is the greatest thing that God can give us; for He himself is love; and it is the greatest thing we can give to God; for it will also give ourselves and carry with it all that is ours." Jeremy Taylor

SAGITTARIUS

Quality	Mutable Light
Element	Fire Spirit
Symbol	Archer, Archer's Arrow
House	Ninth
Ruler	**Jupiter** . . . search for truth, knowledge and enlightenment
Co-Ruler	**Neptune** . . . visions of insight and understanding wisdom
Exaltation Ruler	**Jupiter** . . . expansion of knowledge and truth teachings to inspired spirit manifestation.
Jupiter Glyph	The Jupiter glyph is composed of the moon which astrologically represents ones personality positioned to the East (ascension—I AM identity position) of the cross of earth life experiences. The I AM personality is in a position to direct ones earth experiences, or to be directed from those same experiences.

jupiter Glyph

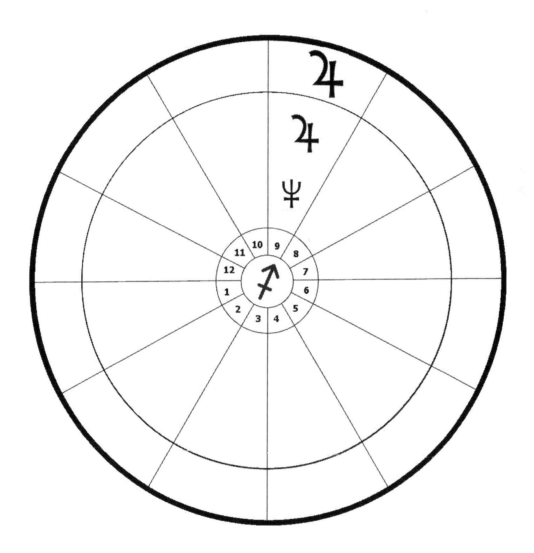

sagittarius chart

SAGITTARIUS

Sagittarius, the mutable fire sign represents the search for spirit (fire) light (mutable) in each one. The Sagittarius symbol is the archer, or archer's arrow, aiming high to attain goals of spirit light—enlightenment from divine Spirit. The archer is depicted as half animal (behind) and half-man (forward) in a poised stance with bow and arrow arched, aimed and ready to "shoot for the stars," bodies of illumination, esoteric Spirit lights. The archer, as each individual, in the process of seeking enlightenment, transforms/ transmutes the body of self to leave the animal self behind, and move ahead, or forward, in and through spirit goal manifestation.

Sagittarius is found in the astrological ninth house of learning and knowledge; the house representing life's philosophies, religion, higher education and distant travels of body and/or mind. In this house one learns of self through one's religion and philosophical perception. Each one literally lives his/her religion. The word religion means to bind together. Ideally, religion teaches a relationship and an awareness of man's unity, binding, with his God. The church is ideally, a meaningful assembly place, where one is taught individual unity with his/her Source and the binding together of all—rather than separation through doctrinal difference. Doctrine is nothing more than man's interpretation or misinterpretation of truths. When churches become crystallized with doctrines, dogmas, edicts, and external rituals, absent of spirit's understanding love and light, they become teachers of darkness, misunderstanding, hate and intolerance. The literal law teachers of the church today, as in the past, are at work pitting man against man, and religion against religion. An individual's beliefs or faith is his or her vision of truth. Truth is found in one's individual Spiritual receptive quest, through studies and exploring, through sincere inquiry and independent search. To earnestly seek is to find. There is an expansion and release through knowledge to one's higher divine mind consciousness. "The kingdom of heaven is within." The Greek word for Heaven is Ouranos, which means expansion. The kingdom of heaven is the infinite presence within; the expanding, unfolding limitless growth of divine consciousness in each soul

"There is an innermost center in us all, where truth abides in fullness, . . . and to know, rather consists in opening out a way whence the imprisoned splendor may escape, than in effecting entry for a light supposed to be without" Robert Browning.

Browning is one of many poets whose beautiful writings manifest spirit light. When one is so inspired (in spirit) there is an in-drawing, absorbing, and assimilating of outer stimuli to a beautiful awareness interpretation. All inspiration comes from divine Spirit. Inspiration is the Spirit at work in every man. The very life in man is Spirit-Life and when man becomes aware in and through his search, he is inspired toward a fulfilling goal of oneness with that inherent life.

Neptune, planetary co-ruler of Sagittarius, assists in adding inspiration, visions of insight and understanding evolved through the wisdom of experience. "From understanding comes wisdom and wisdom is the application of knowledge."(Author unknown)Man is free to know truth and to know error. To know truth there must be an internal change, an upheaval in thought processes, ideas and habits, feelings and attitudes. Human views and opinions must be severed with the sword of truth from a higher level of consciousness. The thoughts and philosophies of each one must be continuously stirred up, separated, weeded out and renewed to un-mix truths from error. Error beliefs and habits of the past must be left in the past. Thoughts can be binding and limiting. Some individuals are so choked with fear emotions and habits of error limitations that new ideas are literally blocked. Each soul is in a different place of receptivity. An open, receptive consciousness nourishes new ideas as they "sink in." Ideas begin to grow and flourish, breaking "inner ground" into "light—awareness." To improve ones quality of life, it is necessary to continuously aim and seek an illumined working order and level of understanding, to contemplate facts from a high Spirit level. The wise man is one who is aware of his inner light spiritual illumination, his Star within. Directed by his star in the heavens, his symbolic enlightened place of consciousness, man becomes the master of his soul.

"Man is his own star, and the soul that can render an honest and perfect man commands all light, all wisdom and all fate." Emerson

Light is the substance of divine spirit in action, working to unfold and expand the consciousness, to transform thoughts of chaos to order, and discern the unreal from the real.

Jupiter, planet of expansion, rules, and is exalted in the sign of Sagittarius. In mythology, Jupiter overthrew and replaced his father Saturn, the mythological god symbolizing karmic earth lesson experiences, to become the father of gods and men. With the assistance of Cyclops (single eye) equated to the straight arrow shooting of the Sagittarius archer, Jupiter knew One Source, One Power, and became master of the world. Through directed, pointed, single eye expansion of consciousness in divine Spirit light, one becomes master of his/her world of earth experiences. Through continuous Jupiter rulership, a conscious expansion growth, transforms the self from karmic life directed experiences, to transmuting Spirit Light directed Jupiter exaltation experiences! The moon of the personality is no longer confined by the material plane. There is an expansion and release through knowledge, to higher divine mind; to one's Spirit-Light, a transforming renewal of the mind. The ruler, Jupiter, transcends knowledge to wisdom, the symbolized expression of Jupiter's exalted rulership.

Each life learns from an ongoing expansion of awareness in light. Some struggle with little light, but at times will feel the helpful vibration of another's light and be motivated to step upward to higher awareness. We are all teachers, we are all students. Each one's life is a lesson by example, to some measure, to each one he encounters. Intentionally or not, we inspire and expand, or hinder awareness in others. We are all children of the same Spirit, learning and growing to manhood.

"There is one great source of all special manifestation of spirit. This spirit is self renewed in each one who will listen, by teachings from within." Emerson

Where Sagittarius is found in one's makeup, as can be seen in an astrology chart (life-map) gives one insight to life area opportunities of individual Spirit Light expansion. The Sagittarius exaltation goal is to live a spirit of truth, to consciously seek, recognize, and expand the Spirit Light in self—then to impersonally, continuously grow in that light so that it will shine, ignite, flame and expand the light in others.

"Look into your own selves and find the spark of truth that God has put in every heart and that only you can kindle to a flame." Socrates

CAPRICORN

Quality	Cardinal Will
Element	Earth Physical.
Symbols	Crocodile, Goat, Unicorn
House	Tenth
Ruler	**Saturn** . . . refining discipline, determination to deepen and perfect character.
Co-Ruler	**Uranus** . . . change of awareness to new level of Will manifestation.
Exaltation Ruler	**Mars** . . . energy projected to high goal purpose and manifestation. Stimulates desire to climb the heights
Mars Glyph . . .	is composed of the cross of the material earth pointed upward and to the right. A projected high aim from one's inner Spirit base.

mars glyph

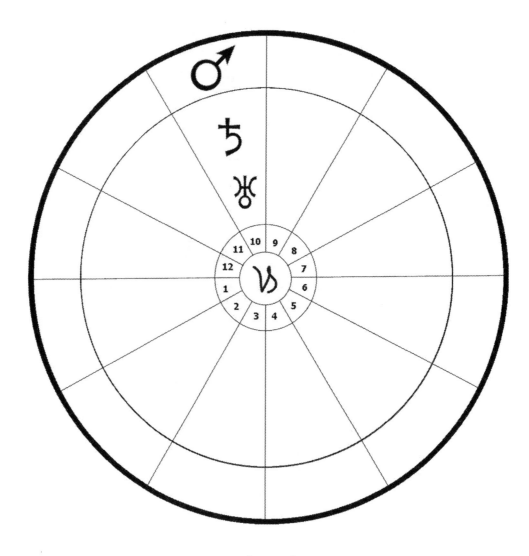

capricorn chart

CAPRICORN

Capricorn, the cardinal earth sign of astrology, demonstrates will (cardinal) manifestation (earth) in each one. The ego will and/or divine Will goals of each individual are physically expressed in Capricorn and can symbolically be seen at work in and through the astrological houses and relationships wherein the sign is individually found. Capricorn is the sign of the tenth house, mid-heaven, apex or highest culminating point, astrologically representing public recognition, career and goals. It is the noon position where one demonstrates will impersonally to others in the summit of full sunlight. The tenth house is the final house of will expression, where the goal is to ultimately relinquish ego will to divine Will.

Saturn, planetary ruler of Capricorn is also the ruler of earth form. It is symbolically the great karmic law teacher which disciplines and molds the ego will through lessons of self-discipline, responsibility and limitation, to alignment with the higher divine Will of self. Each one struggles with karmic cause and effect experiences, wrestling human self with "high-self." Man lives each life taking different parts and roles, facing and wrestling with each situation on the earth plane, living lives-roles toward the innate goal of perfection of self "All the worlds a stage and all men become merely players." Shakespeare.

Saturn strengthens one through concentrated energy influencing endurance, introspection, stability and self discipline—all qualities essential to deepen and perfect character. The Capricorn symbol of the goat represents the tenacious one ever striving, struggling, and climbing upward. Another symbol, the sea-goat (in some legends the crocodile) representing the overcoming from the depths of self (the inner-soul foundation level) reflected from Cancer's opposition sign of emotional will, to the heights of self, exhibited in Capricorn's outer manifestation, physical will. Man moves on the earth plane of experience slowly evolving upward through ego will to divine Will struggles. "That aim in life is highest which requires the highest and finest discipline." Henry Thoreau

The "scapegoat" is the sacrificial goat or lower nature of man that is in time, sacrificed and awakened to one's higher sacred nature. The word sacrifice comes from the root "sacri," which does not mean to kill, but does mean to make "whole-holy," sacred. Through struggle experiences, the soul is able to make tremendous growth progress. Many of the experiences of life are painful and difficult; some are labeled bad. A bad experience in one's life may be the stimulus-goad to force one to move forward toward the ultimate good direction of divine Will power goals.

Uranus, co-ruling planet of Capricorn assists to bring realization awareness of inner Will presence. Each one must become consciously aware of the Presence within before that Presence can be made manifest. With awareness, one is in a position to observe and judge his/her life progress; to become one's own judge and jury as he/she becomes aware from the cause and effect, action-reaction laws of life. We are not punished for our sins of error, which are unaware, "missing-the mark" experiences, but by them, an automatic correction of karmic law in action. According to one's deeds is one's punishment or reward. The Saturn—Uranus influence teaches one to judge and observe insightfully the fruits evident as manifested in one's life. If the "cause" seeds sown have produced "effect" fruits of anxiety, sickness, lack and limitation, it is important to plant new goal seeds of strength and peace. Each day is a judgment day but also a day of sowing. Each individual is of divine seed, and must eventually grow and produce in kind. The divine Will seed in each one will always produce good, as the ceaseless, continuous, energy power Will of the Creator fulfilling each creation.

The Unicorn, also recognized as a symbol of Capricorn, would represent the exaltation expression of one who climbs to high mountain summits aiming and projecting from the soul's single-eye position with determined directed one—pointedness, as does Capricorn's exalted ruler Mars. Mars, represents the initiating, goal oriented primal force principle of individual self assertion to express the self through projected goals. The Mars glyph is composed of the cross of the material earth pointed upward and to the right. A projected high aim directed from Spirit base. Symbolically, Mars in Capricorn exaltation points the cross of the physical will directed from Spirit Will energy to aspiring goals of public action. It is important that one's goals be of clear motive and sincerity of purpose, as a strong inner desire-force will attract, draw as a magnet, the deep soul desire in each to be whole; to fulfill areas of life not complete and to draw to the self, needed experience to do so. Mars has been called the planet of war. If man's ego will is striving for personal interests of ambition, power, and status public image only, there is a conflict or war with self and others. Truly its misuse would prove to be its own detriment and/or fall. The Mars self-will ego energy of warring with ones error limitations, glamour's and illusions can be transferred from wasted energy to productive motivating goal setting energy. This transfer of goals, with purity of interest, through mature constructive channels, directs one to new altruistic horizons of experience. The unselfish high-goal energy directed from the courage and conviction of divine Will consciousness is active energy; devoted to aid the welfare of others, while presenting one with rewards of great growth through meeting and overcoming life's difficult challenges. To unfold and manifest one's inner-glory is to become—to Be the Presence in action. This is the ultimate physical plan-action goal, the Capricorn exalted mission, to physically glorify and project divine Will in purpose and manifestation.

> "A person who impoverishes his body with the idea that it is only the spirit that counts, displays as warped a view of truth as the man who starves and neglects the spirit and cares only for the body. In god's plan the development should progress in harmonious order, with equally divided attention. The spirit requires a noble instrument in order to carry out the full Will of God." Henry B. Wilson

AQUARIUS

Quality	Fixed Love
Element	Air Mental
Symbol	Water Bearer
House	Eleventh
Ruler:	**Uranus** . . . new awareness and perception of self in relation to others.
Co-Ruler:	**Saturn** . . . responsibility to society. Self love sacrifice.
Exaltation Ruler:	**Venus** . . . unconditional love, acceptance of others, brotherly love based on understanding devotion to humanitarian goals of harmony and unity. Agape love
Venus Glyph . . .	is symbolically composed of Spirit exalted over the cross of matter.

venus glyph

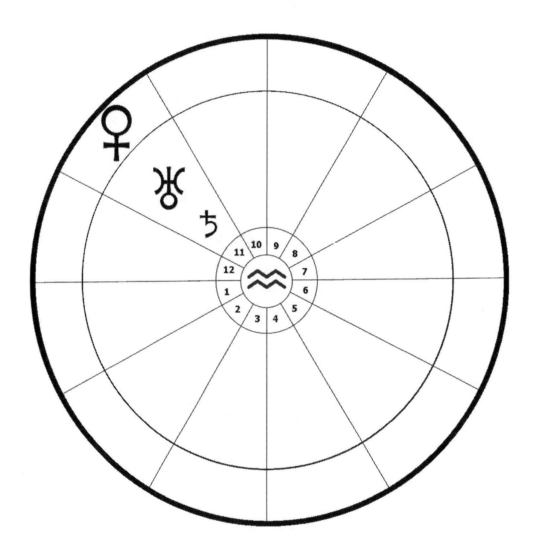

aquarius chart

AQUARIUS

Aquarius, the fixed air-sign of man, exemplifies the mental (air) love (fixed) purpose to be fulfilled in and through mankind. Mental love is a detached caring view of another or others. The Aquarius glyph represents life's vital energy—living, loving thought waves in expression. The Aquarian water bearer symbolically represents the "man aware" who carries forth pure emotional-psychological (water) truths spreading, pouring them to flow freely to the all of humanity. This emotional water is symbolic of the love ideas-thoughts activated and carried forth by man from the Pisces age teachings of love. Erroneous concepts of misunderstandings, hates, and prejudices are as unclean muddy, bitter water. An unenlightened man is one needing clear living-water spiritual truth. Aquarius is the water-bearer, carrying electrifying, energizing "'living water," psychological understanding of truth from an intellectual and emotional love depth of insight and vision. To know and feel, be alive, to this water, this mental-love understanding level of living truth, man must be made aware.

Uranus, the ruler of Aquarius, is the breakthrough planet expressing awareness and perception of Self in relation to others. Uranus directs an individual to approach life's social group relationships, (defined in the eleventh house of Aquarius,) with new, open awareness and understandings. The Uranus influence instigates the breaking up of old attitudes, crystallized expressions, rigid views, prejudices and dividing thoughts to re-think, to review, so that new enlightened levels of awareness can be realized.

Aquarius is the astrological sign representing freedom and independence. Life's upheaval experience lessons bring change, instigating independence. The personal attachment relationships in one's life, induce a familiar, routine, habit of security, even when the relationship is miserable. It is often easier to stick with a bad situation that is known, than to make change and grow in and through the unknown. So one allows the self to be fixed or locked in to difficult emotional relationship experiences until the Uranus influence of upheaval and change forces one to move and grow. Even seemingly good relationships of comfortable routine can stifle and limit one to a narrow sphere of attitudes and relationships revolving around the ego-self. The Uranus transits bring the many necessary lessons of disruptive change, e.g., spouse or children leaving home, death of loved ones, natural or physical disasters as fires, hurricane, disease, or the unexplained personal deep-feeling need to escape, to "be free." All change brings growth. Through the lessons of helplessness, feeling completely alone, one develops the strength of independence—which evolves, in time to dependence from within—security from the inner Source of one's being, the divine omnipresent life Source of each and all. A truly independent individual is one who is aware of, and bases his dependence on his or her Source. To transfer from the personal to the universal, fulfills great realization of individuality. Each person is uniquely individual, yet each functions from the same life Source. The evolved aware one understands, and knows "unity in diversity."

Saturn, the co-ruling planet of Aquarius, aids and disciplines in man a positive, physical karmic law responsibility to self and society. To be free of rigid relationship attitudes by choosing right use (righteousness) of interaction, one releases the ego-self to the impersonal higher Self-one self consciousness. "The Son's of Man are One." To realize the Aquarian goal of one-self consciousness, it is necessary to exhibit mental-love—"agape love" to all of humanity projected from an impersonal, detached, intellectual, caring relationship.

Venus is the planetary exaltation ruler of the impersonal love sign Aquarius. The Venus glyph is symbolically composed of spirit exalted over the cross of matter. Divine Spirit fulfills, overcomes, and transcends karmic law matter experiences through love. Spirit is exalted above the cross of material consciousness. Love carries an emotional perceptibility, an insight (seeing from within) as avatars of different creeds have and do carry to show the way of loving brotherhood to all men. Truth has been taught and expressed as love by "Christed" ones in all races and throughout all religions.

The eleventh house of relationships, hopes and wishes for the future and social security, symbolically represents the future security goals of mankind which can and will be realized through an agape love, a self sacrificing love, freely given from the divine Love Source of one's being. Agape Love evokes a detached transcending expression of harmony, tolerance and understanding based on right relationships of all mankind.

Venus rules beauty and the beautiful. In its exalted high form, one sees in others and expresses in self an intangible inner beauty which stems from a loving soul. As one sees beauty in others, he/she has called forth the beauty and love in self. To be able to see and know the unity in all, lifts the consciousness to an impersonal high agape-love level of understanding. In the absence of this awareness, man symbolically expresses an unintended detriment of Venus, blindly reacting to the influences of prejudice, hate, and narrow vision, as would humanity's small child in darkness on a low step of life's ladder to divinity. Each one climbs, evolves through the stages and steps of love, beginning and ending with personal love security (Taurus) to love of one's personal creation-child (Leo) love of and for another (Scorpio) to Aquarian love, a fulfilling of the one great law understood and echoed through all creeds—"that ye love others, as self."

To become the son of God, the son of man must pour the Aquarian water of life-living energy, mental-love, into right relationships of understanding and devotion, to the betterment and interests of others; accepting each one at his or her own level and rate of growth, and, accepting collectively all humanity in an impersonal unconditional agape-love. This is the Aquarian exaltation goal. The high realization goals for the future of mankind will be achieved through Love, the perfect cohesive bond of harmony and unity. The Aquarian age of the water, love—bearer, is upon us. It is morning, and the dawn is breaking.

"We are all surrounded by the uniting of Love, there is but one Center from which all species issue, as rays from a Sun." Giordano Bruno, Italian Philosopher.

"No virtue is higher than love to all men, and there is no loftier aim in life than to do good to all men." Confucius.

PISCES

Quality	Mutable Light
Element	Water Emotional
Symbol	Fish
House	Twelfth
Ruler:	**Neptune** . . . emotional depth of insight, inspiration, and intuitive sensitivity.
Co-Ruler:	**Jupiter** . . . vision expansion of optimism and faith.
Exaltation:	Ruler **Mercury** . . . light communicator, impressionable sensitivity perception, understanding humility. idealism, vision, wisdom.

Mercury Glyph . . . symbolically shows a receptivity of soul personality, rested on spirit exalted over the cross of matter.

mercury glyph

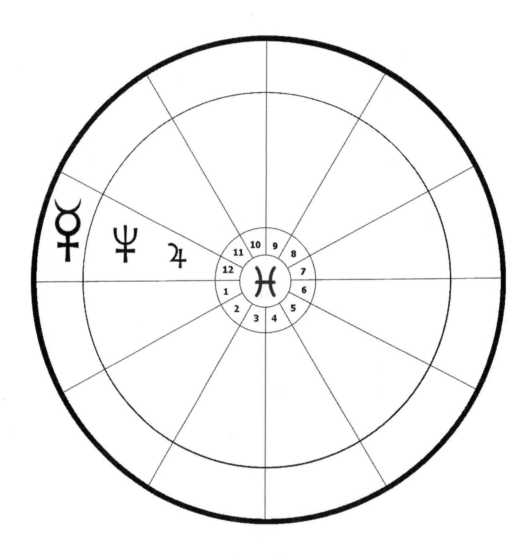

pisces chart

PISCES

Pisces is the mutable water sign of emotional (water) light (mutable). Emotional light is an inherent harvest of wisdom, which is present in each one waiting to gradually unfold through objective understandings of emotional experience relationships. The deep emotional waters of one's being are the emotional experience relationship memories contained in the psyche or soul of self. The "deep waters" below the surface of outer physical expression hold the secret and hidden subconscious thoughts and feelings in each individual. The Pisces symbol is the fish, which symbolically dwells and swims in one's emotional thoughts or subconscious waters of the soul. The Pisces glyph is composed of two Moon symbols, representing the personality, facing two opposing directions—linked and connected in balance. The two directions represent the inner-outer, subconscious-conscious levels of self. The outer personality expression is tied to, and surfaced from, the psychological emotional thinking level of self. The Pisces expression is also, symbolically, two fold in function as positive-negative and action-reaction.

The twelfth house, where the Pisces sign and symbol reside, is the house of ones personal harvest of understandings. The, symbolic, fish duality of emotional feelings, thoughts, ideas and visions of the inner-self, will determine the conscious harvest expressed from one's level of personal understanding. One's deep, secret hidden thoughts can represent an undesirable harvest of personal confinement: of self undoing through negative thoughts and/or unexpressed emotions of worries, fears, doubts, illusions, self deceptions and personal confusion; all traits which might be labeled expressions of the Pisces ruler influence Neptune, planet of deep emotional waters. One's negative thoughts and feelings are the self created dark, hidden secret enemies of one's being. Each individual must live according to his or her beliefs. Emotional thoughts are beliefs which create after their own kind. It is not enough to want to believe in good "I believe, help my unbelief." An anxious concern or worry is unbelief, is a fear which stops—blocks the free love-light flow of the divine energy Source from within.

Positive thoughts and beliefs are as treasures in one's consciousness, releasing the flow of good into the life. Neptune's symbolic positive ruler influence brings insight, inspiration, and intuitive sensitivity. Jupiter's positive planetary co-ruling influence adds inner expansion and depth of soul searching, through qualities of optimism, charity, faith and aspiration. The combined positive Neptune-Jupiter influence stimulates one's self-understanding evolution to a high level place of self. The "upper room" consciousness of the soul; a place where one in secret communion-union with the source of his being, fulfills the deep yearning to link the ego-self with the divine and is able to transform intellect and knowledge to understanding wisdom. In this inner place of the soul, one knows there are "no things"—nothing to-fear. When a thing is understood, the mystery of fear, the negativity or darkness has been exposed through the ever-present, ever-flowing communication of Light. The three Pisces ruling planets are Jupiter-co-ruler, Neptune-ruler, and Mercury, exultation ruler; all work together as a necessary combination in the soul's development to understanding.

"In Jupiter's forces, we find those great ennobling elements, those conditions that would bring the forces of good in life. In Neptune, those of mysticism, mystery, spiritual insight and spiritual development. The Mercury influence of mental understanding of each. Then with the mental insight into the operative elements of ennobling of virtues, of good, of beautiful, with the mysteries of the universal forces, given understanding, brings the development to soul's forces . . . . For the soul feeds upon that environment to which the mental guides and directs." Edgar Cayce Reading; No.900-14.

Mercury, the impersonal carrier planet of light sensitivity, finds its highest expression, exaltation in Pisces, impersonal sign of emotional light reflecting from the twelfth house of self-understanding and wisdom; the impersonal harvest of emotional and mental images purified and refined in divine light. Mercury, the mythological winged messenger of God, the divine receiver-communicator, is symbolized by receptivity of soul personality resting on spirit, exalted over the cross of matter. Mercury in Pisces exaltation, represents an intuitive knowing, impressionable receptivity perceptive-reflection link between the soul and personality. From the highest level of communication, wisdom of the "Light Source" within, the Light Life Source of one's being, the omniscient presence is always shining, always waiting to be received to beam through to conscious connection. When the outer body senses are at rest as in quiet meditation or in sleep, the soul is ever alert and alive, and able to communicate with the inner guiding, instructing higher-self, impressing and teaching through dreams and dream symbols. The quality of thought before sleep will determine the quality of dream instructions. If the mind is cluttered with worries and fears before sleep, much of that state would be carried into the dream as confusion and anxiety blocking one's pure inner light expression. Before sleeping, it is important to make an effort mentally to consciously remove burdens of the mind as one would physically remove outer clothing from the body. Quiet the mind, read some inspirational poetry or literature, and consciously make an effort to prepare the self for sleep by clearing-cleansing the mind to the freeing indwelling presence of light. Image light, before sleep or in quiet meditation, to release and free the mind from all outer thoughts transcending reason. Envision light freely flowing, warmly radiating everywhere so that when in illumined consciousness, one may then ponder—question a thing, and know; may experience a pure light revelation of understanding. One can only receive wisdom, a true insight of vision from an inner enlightened level of communication. Vision is man's wish, prophecy of intention to be fulfilled. If one images-imagines a thing, and desires or loves it long enough, he will in time, live or manifest it. Unenlightened, unaware man, from the lessons of misuse of communication, painfully learns the bondage of human ignorance and darkness of the ego-self; "We cannot comprehend ruin until we are ourselves in ruin." Heinrich Heine

The soul evolves "'to know," to communicate true images and desires, the action must be expressed in kind. If the desire is to receive love, the action must be loving—to emotionally shine outward to all, not to think love to self, but from self. Free caring light radiating out towards others, is automatically drawn to its warmth as a love magnet effect. A pulling or drawing to self as "love-me" cause action, will affect retraction. If the desire is receiving, the action must be giving. And so the perceptive antenna to the intuitive inner level of vision can come to anyone receiving, as communicating from the inner light of being. Light represents understanding. When one understands, he/she is saved or released from the bondages of false beliefs and of human ignorance. "Everyone hears only what he understands." Johann Van Goethe.

The self is free to see, hear and know, is free to choose right use of vision. All things increase-improve with use. Wisdom is the result of wise choices and continuous use of following divine intelligence, choosing that which is impersonally beneficial to all. The knowing-light each one carries will awaken him/her to inner awareness to know the self. When one can truly know the Self, he/she can communicate with, and understand another.

"This, above all; to thine own self be true and it must follow, as the night the day, than canst not then be false to any man." William Shakespeare.

The power to communicate belongs to the soul transmitted through the body to others for divine purpose. Each individual is at one with his source to consciously understand, know that all life carries light in some measure. The exalted Piscean goal is to emotionally understand, accept each one with kindness and compassion, caring impersonally, without judgment of others, accepting each where they are in experience and understanding. It is to no longer put certain ones on a pedestal, or feel disappointment in others; as the knowing vision sees, there is always an underlying high plan at work in and through the life and action of each and all.

Pisces rules the feet which symbolize the foundation on which one stands—"takes his stand"—ones under-standing base. It is important to purify our foundation of understanding of one another. If one's Mercury sensory antenna is exalted to a place where human life can be seen through purity of insight, see the self reflected in others, see a unity of all life; then one is standing on a high consciousness level of truth, an understanding of good at work, gathering, harvesting, uniting in the each and all of life.

ARIES

Quality	Cardinal Will
Element	Fire Spirit
Symbol	Ram
House	First
Ruler	**Pluto** . . . personal resurrection; bursting forth into new Spirit Life awareness.
Co-Ruler:	**Mars** . . . self assertion action; initial survival, energy force.
Exaltation Ruler	**Sun** . . . Spirit identity—"I AM" realization, personal spirit life force.
Sun Glyph . . .	is the circle of infinity, the uncontained, without boundary, primal power spirit, without beginning or end. The dot in the center represents the life seed focus made manifest.

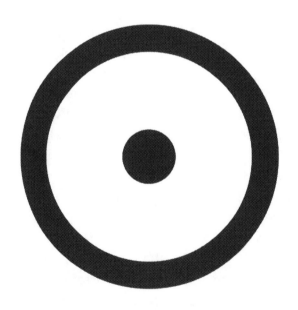

sun glyph

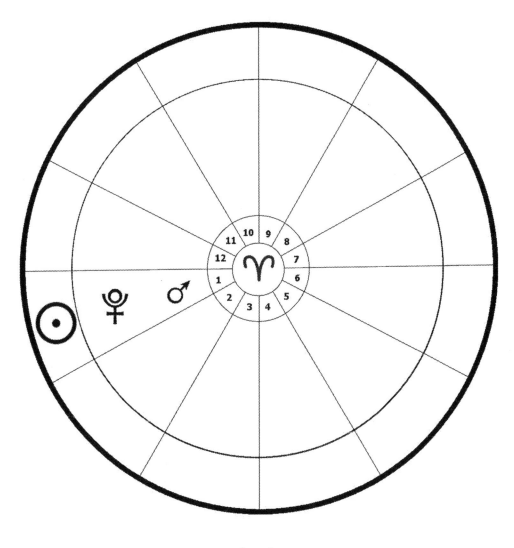

aries chart

ARIES

Aries, the cardinal fire sign establishes the combined trait of spirit (fire) will (cardinal) in expression. There is an individual spirit, will-power presence, present in each life which is put to action as free will choice. This individual power while freely used by man comes from the One divine Spirit Will, the life power source of and in all things. Within all and each life expression is the creative activating life principle of all that life may become. Within each individual soul is also the root and seed of all he or she may become, a blueprint of perfection.

Aries, the self-expressing pioneer sign of the zodiac, appears in the astrological first house-ascendant or horizon point of life. The first house represents the new beginning place, a place of personal self-identity and manifested physical appearance—a symbolic representative of man's appearance in form or expression in matter. As a new seed underground breaks forth on the horizon to new life manifestation, so also must man give life to the spirit within. In a conscious outer expression, spirit and matter begin to perform as one unit.

Pluto, resurrection planet and Ruler of Aries, represents the personal resurrection in man; the personal identity in action, bursting forth into new life. This new life message is and has been celebrated by man annually in many creeds, rituals and festivals, including the Christian Easter. In the Aries spring season. calendars record the time of Easter, Christian resurrection celebration, as the first Sunday following the first full moon (time of greatest light) of the Vernal-Spring Equinox. In the spring, life form breaks the husks of winter, as symbolically, the divine inner will of man breaks forth to new life—new birth. The egg hatches from the shell—the will breaks through personal self-image in a struggle to begin anew. The seed of self breaks through again and again from one life to another, from one zodiac sign to another, from one cycle of self to another, even a daily cycle. The physical body is constantly renewed by partial death. Old cells die, new ones are created replacing them; and so it goes cycle after cycle, until that time when man lives fully in Spirit.

Pluto, the planet of death and new life, portrays the wonderful resurrection message of continuous life. There is no spiritual death; there is only physical death. The soul of life in each and all is continually evolving and growing through the physical processes of birthing, living, and dying; until it is no longer necessary for physical manifestation. Final death to the physical sends the living soul onward—forward to new levels of life experiences beyond the physical.

Mars, planetary co-ruler of Aries, projects a self assertion "me-first" initial energy burst of human life. The Mars influence stimulates a self motivated survival force of energy which, with steadfast purpose, pushes one forward and upward to new growth experiences in and through the many areas and levels of life. Mars directly points the way to spirit breakthrough.

The Aries age was one of great darkness, of individual struggle for identity in a low place of humanity's gradual evolution of life. Prophets and wise men living in the age, as Abraham and Moses, found it necessary to teach the people identity truths through literal symbolic action and demonstration commandments. Truths were etched in stone and could only be understood and followed on a very basic literal level. The ram or lamb, symbol of Aries physically, represented the resurrection truth in the only way that could be understood. Death of one life form for another-.the sacrificial ram was literally burned on an altar, representing mans surrender or death of the lower animal (physical) self through the spiritual fire "Spirit-fire" of purity, or, man made whole, made sacred through a new resurrection of life in Spirit. The Jewish religion still employs the ram's horn symbol of that time and cycle.

Near the end of the Aries cycle, another avatar of the age, Jesus, often called the good shepherd, taught "feed my sheep" and literally demonstrated, in this Aries age of personal identity, himself as the "sacrificial lamb." He died on the physical cross (cross represents earth manifestation) showing literal physical body death to the souls new resurrected Spirit body. This literal symbolic demonstration was to teach that each one must die—sacrifice physical human will of self in order to live in Spirit-Will.

Aries symbolically shows each one, as can be seen in ones individual chart, areas of opportunity to pass from the human ego level of self to a higher divine Spirit level of expression. The resurrection of Jesus symbolically ended the Aries age cycle and heralded a new Pisces age of Christianity, to a new life cycle, to begin an understanding of this Spirit in man. The Pisces fish symbol is also the symbol of Christianity.

From the all-originating first principal Spirit, comes substance; substance is God-energy. God energy, identity is the "I Am" from which all things manifest and are brought to focus in form. The Creator is always greater than the created; the Creator is the life in all things. The creator-presence in man, is the power, the presence, the mind, the life, and the power above all, through all, and in all; it is the goal of each man to know the Source, the "I Am" origin of his being. "and God created man in his own image" Genesis 1:27 (I AM age) the personal identification of the Spirit in man is his "I AM" life presence, called the very name of the creator.

"I AM THAT I AM" Exodus 3:14. Each one must recognize his Source; each and no other is capable of declaring his individual "I am." The I AM life presence reality is always in man.

"Oh man, know thyself. In thee is hid the treasure of treasures!" Hermetic Maxim.

The Sun, exaltation ruler of Aries, is the energy source center of planet Earth and the physical life and forms there-in. The Sun is always shining as, is the "I AM" center in man. To feel and see and know that continuous presence, man must lift his/her own dark clouds of ignorance; when this is done, the personal spirit will—I am ego identity can be clearly seen and thus overcome, to the full Will, energy and light of the shining Spirit within. The unlimited potential, the seed can at last be brought to fulfilling, conscious focus development in one's life.

The astrological glyph representing the Sun is composed of the circle of infinity the uncontained, without boundary, primal power Spirit, without beginning or end. The dot in the center represents the life seed focus made manifest.

The Sun is the source center of one's universe, and symbolically of one's being. The Spirit guided individual is in touch with his/her source and thus has a deep sense of purpose. One so in touch is led by this Spirit Will source as a channel of divine energy, quietly, confidently meeting obstacles, defying and overcoming life's great and small challenges, from a new focus of vital Spirit Power.

The Aries exaltation goal is to personally "know" and fulfill one's intense desire to manifest Spirit Will identity: to let "Divine Will be done in and through me," to develop a deep sense of purpose and direction, to make right use of this wonderful (full of One—filled with One) energy. The Sun shines-expresses, in and through right action. When the Sun (Son) of man, human ego-spirit will, descends, the Sun (Son) of the omnipotent Creator ascends. The Sun (Son) shines in full-light of his/her Spirit Will and knows the "I AM" source of being. The physical appearance will radiate with the divine aura-halo. At the time, when all of mankind recognizes his Sun-"SON-ship" from the Leo birth (astrologically ruled by the Sun and exalted in Pluto) to the maturity of new birth in Spirit, personal I AM realization, Aries, (astrologically ruled by Pluto and exalted in the Sun), then, in that day and time . . . shall there be serenity and peace in man: "And the Lion (Leo)shall lie down with the lamb" (Aries)

TAURUS

Quality	Fixed Love
Element	Physical Earth
Symbol	Bull
House	Second
Ruler:	**"X"** . . . very personal intimate love presence in each. wholeness/ holiness security.
Co-Ruler:	**Venus** . . . to sense harmony, love and beauty in all.
Exaltation Ruler:	**Moon** . . . to reflect and project one's divine inner love source presence to and through outer personality expression.
Moon Glyph . . .	a crescent moon symbolizing the personality of the Soul. A reflection of the sun as the earth's moon in light, reflects the sun.

moon glyph

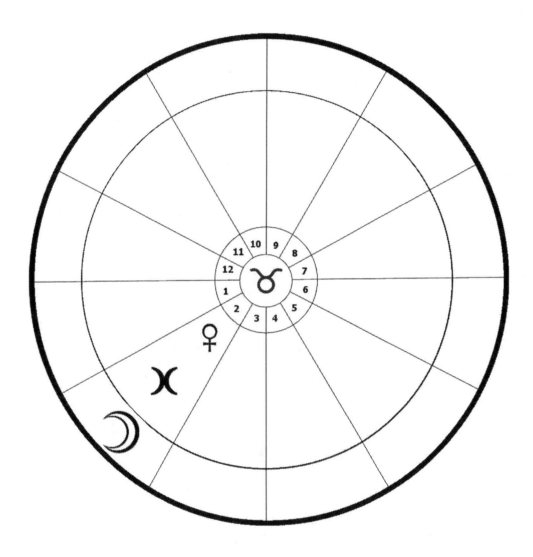

taurus chart

TAURUS

Taurus, the Earth (physical) sign of the zodiac, symbolically expresses the love (fixed) presence within man personally brought forth into physical body manifestation.

One's physical body is the substance expressing, reflecting, and molded by ones personal soul consciousness. Substance is "God Stuff," all manifestation has origin in and from the divine creative energy source. Man has been given the power of personal soul growth through the use of his omnipotent Source. The right use of this Source will manifest an inner-security, a soul contentment in all of its fullness.

The Taurus sign, the bull and astrological house position (second,) represent the personal life securities of each one. The Taurean Age (around 4000-2000 B.C) was a time when man worshipped the golden calf (bull), figurative symbol of form and rich physical security possessions. The Taurus bull represents the animal level security found in and through man's treasures and earth attachments. The lessons of the earth are many; while some display application through possessiveness, self-indulgence and the craving for food and luxury; (all security lessons,) in time, will teach right use of practical, beneficial application, as those of inner-strength, reliability, patience, endurance, stability, determination and a solid set of values—all Taurus characteristics.

The second house of Taurus represents physical expression securing the self identity of first house image, through ones possessions. Possessions in and of themselves cannot be labeled good or bad. With right use, man is in the divine flow of automatic abundant supply. Inner security can be found in an environment void of material possessions or in an environment abundant with material possessions. Possessions, things, can never be a cause of true inner security, only a result. The personal challenge of material holdings is that one may often let possessions posses him/her. One who would still figuratively worship the "golden calf" is one who becomes emotionally dependent on, a literal love for physical value things as a measure of security. Material riches can never truly satisfy; they are the physical securities vulnerable to loss, destruction and decay. Spiritual riches are the inner-security possessions and treasures as true values of self held in the soul.

> "Remember that what you possess in this world will he found on the day of your death to belong to somebody else. But what you are will he yours forever" . . . .
> Henry Van Dyke.

True security must be established through a divine love consciousness. This consciousness secures fulfilling abundance. Symbol "X" exemplifies what I believe to be the ruling influence of Taurus, a very personal high vibrational love presence influencing each one. A vibration of love similar to that of Venus, the co-ruler of Taurus, but felt and expressed from a personal intimate level. The loving balanced Christed Source of ones being, "closer than breathing, nearer than hands and feet" is this personal love awareness which has been carried by great avatars and teachers of all religions. This personal love awareness inner-security acknowledgement physically expresses and carries the divine love fulfillment potential within each one. Taurus is the personal love sign. One must be personally secure, loving self, before he/she can be loving to others. Love is the motivating power of the universe. Divine Love continually pours out to all, always present, never ceasing—only to be received. The love source of one's being is always present, giving of vital energy substance—Spirit treasure to manifest to life.

Love is a giving; it is impossible to hold in love. As one contacts the loving source within through many channels as meditation, joy, appreciation and gratitude for the harmony and beauty of ones surroundings and circumstances, he/she contacts life's giving love flow; and in so doing, becomes a loving giver. One possesses and expresses peaceful inner-security through the act of giving.

Venus, the love planet of beauty and harmony, co-ruling Taurus, aids and influences man to see and be beauty. To see love, releases inner feelings of reverence and gratitude to the Creator and to others. Love moves through Venus expressions of joyful music, beautiful arts and poetry. Beauty within the consciousness creates desire to be surrounded by beauty and the beautiful. Love desire as highly expressed in Venus, attracts the beautiful and good. To see beauty is to love. Love assists one in seeing the inner-beauty presence in each one. In seeing love, one becomes loving and through the act of loving, transforms the inner-beauty of the self to a radiant, outer beautiful physical love manifestation.

"In all the universe there is no greater power than the power of God's love, no greater security than the security of his love, no greater riches . . . than that which is yours, . . . in the love that enfolds you, even the love of the infinite." Clara Palmer.

The Moon exaltation of Taurus and astrological symbol of personality represents the personality goal of each one to reflect and project the inner divine love to outer manifestation. The Taurus glyph is composed of the Moon symbol of personality lifted and exalted upon Spirit base. (see Taurus chart center) Personality rests in an exalted position upon the foundation of spiritual power. The Moon reflects the Sun. The outer personality reflects the inner Spirit. When one can see and love from the divine love-light Source within, the true self-the soul becomes integrated and the human self, outer mask personality, becomes the reflection of that deep, personal love vibration, symbolized by "X;" The outer ego-animal emotional nature is overcome, transformed; there is a symbolic unveiling, de-masking, to and through divine personality.

"The Soul is not where it lives but where it loves." H. G. Bohn

From the security found in and from one's personal divine inner-love Source, one will know true values and will reflect a beautiful, radiant, outer-form personality manifestation of Love—the Taurus exaltation goal of true security success.

"Men attract not that which they want, but that which they are." James Allen

"Success lies very largely in our own hands. It means effort; it means having a definite aim and striving earnestly to achieve it; it means wise planning, a knowledge of our-self, of our circumstances and possibilities; It means the power to judge truly of values." Grenviille Kleiser

GEMINI

Quality	Mutable Air
Element	Mental Light
Symbol	Twins
House	Third
Ruler:	**"Z"** . . . personal communication, intuitive connection, inner teacher.
Co-Ruler:	**Mercury** . . . outer communication, conscious connection, investigative.
Exaltation Ruler:	**"Z"** . . . transcending through inner light voice communication to personal communication . . . enlightening; all knowing guiding light source Holy Ghost.
Exaltation Glyph	**"Z"** . . . represents the mental light potential to be fulfilled in man.

glyph z

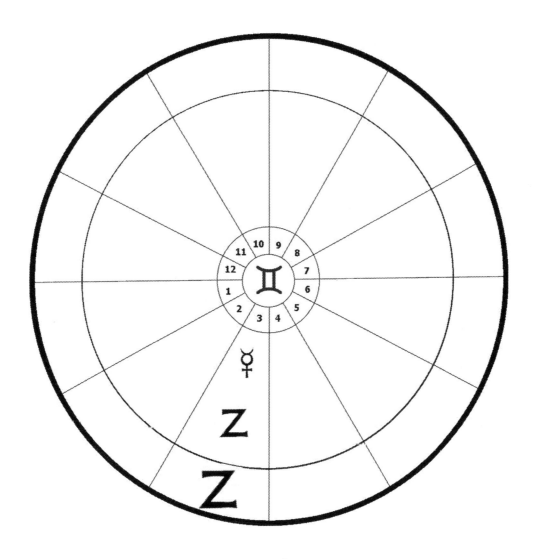

gemini chart

GEMINI

Gemini is the astrological sign of mutable air which portrays the quality of mental (air) light (mutable,) a very personal inner level of "knowing" communication. Gemini is found in the third house of communications. The third house represents the inner teacher—the teacher of self. Each one communicates to self and others what he knows or what he doesn't know, from his or her personal inner, mental-light thinking level.

The outer communication of one's ideas, thoughts and views to others in the form of speaking, teaching, writing and expressions through the various art forms, assist one to visibly see and then, as in playback, communicate from self back to self.

Mercury, the co-ruling "impersonal messenger" communication planet, assists conscious investigative thought movement to outer communicative expression. The thoughts and words one uses can build or destroy. Thoughts are acting, building power forces which create and outwardly manifest. What one believes is his created reality. For example, whatever the weather, if my mind sings, "today is beautiful," it indeed is! Optimism leads to positive results.

"There is nothing either good or had, but thinking makes it: so." William Shakespeare.

"There are glimpses of heaven in every act, or thought, a word that raises us above ourselves." Arthur P. Stanley

Pessimism also manifests in kind. One has dominion of his world through his/her view of the world, to name or interpret everything according to his or her understanding. There is a mind-action law: "Like attracts like," "'Like begets like," "Thoughts held in mind produce after their kind." The thought seeds sown today will produce the experience crops to be harvested tomorrow. Law is the logical and orderly process of omniscient, infinite Light, expressing and moving in and through man.

"A man is the sum total of his thoughts" Buddha.

The twins, symbol of mutable air sign Gemini, represent the mental duality of man. There is an impressionable, changeable, intellectual gatherer of knowledge-mind which communicates and becomes aware through the outer senses of seeing, touching, hearing, smelling and tasting. This sense-mind is often in error, literally limited by mental process; and yet many individuals consciously function and communicate at this level only. There is another "mental sense," an inner level of knowing which can clear the mind of limitations, enlighten the intellect and ponder, reflect, from ones omniscient Source of great inner truth. The Gemini twins face in two directions, and yet, are united as one.

There is a very personal high vibration of light energy within each one; an intuitive connection which defines united Gemini communication in action This influence, represented by the symbol "Z," expresses and communicates in a dual rulership influence. As the Ruler of Gemini, "Z" represents the mental light potential in man to be fulfilled. As the exaltation ruler, it carries a transcending force and vibration to identity awareness and fulfillment. The Z glyph portrays an alternating current, advancing—retreating in duality of expression. "Z" is also a symbol of lightning (enlightening;) portraying rapid motion without solid shape or form, as moving quicksilver, or thoughts in motion. "Z" has long been the symbol of moving quick thought-brainstorms: Eureka!, connections. Z is also the symbol of Omega, the end before another beginning. Gemini is the final personal sign preceding the nadir, or "new beginning" base.

The Z vibratory influence is similar to Gemini's co-ruler planet Mercury, as it is also the communicator, but expressed on a much more personal level, as that "knowing light"—"holy ghost" breath of the supreme Source, given to guide all men. It should be interpreted as a place in one's life, an opportunity, to make contact with, be guided by, one's Omniscient all-knowing Source. Opportunities can be made aware through understanding application of the Gemini position(s) in an individual chart. For example: Gemini on the fifth house cusp would interpret through the creative sources, or children in one's life, an opportunity to develop and release inner knowing, ruler expression.

On an exalted level of expression one would transcend the developed inner-level to be creative from one's divine Omniscient Center If, for example, he or she expressed creativity through poetry, the words would flow from that deep inspired (in spirit) center. Then, looking to Mercury, co-ruler, and its position, sign and aspects, for outer communication opportunities, this might be a way or channel to express one's inspired creation to others. Another example might be: if Mercury is found in the tenth house in the sign of Sagittarius, one would have an opportunity to publicly recite and expand one's philosophy through poetry or to make a career of publishing one's philosophy through poetry.

The "Z" vibration through Gemini rulership works as a personal internal teacher, assisting one to look within and "know." It draws the intuitive "hunch" and/or psychic extrasensory, paranormal experiences in all levels and expressions; through such intuitive experiences, teaches one to re-think, to change error thoughts and ideas to discerning concepts and understandings. Light draws to itself to bring visible order from disorder and confusion of intellectual and subconscious thinking. Divine ideas take shape; the self uses the mind-intellect wisely, and becomes aware of his/her own inner light; thus dissipating dark clouds of error thought.

As one moves to the light, the shadows fall behind; the higher Mind in each is an all-encompassing, constant, ever-present resource containing all of the knowledge and wisdom of the ages. One cannot reach or know, his/her source of inner-knowledge truth until he/she is ready. The sight of the eye is not equal to the intuitive sight of the Spirit. Inner knowledge is spiritual discernment—higher understanding. Truth must be seen by man from Omniscient Spirit Light, symbolized by "Z" exaltation rulership. It is through the channel of one's divine immanent light presence that the expansion of consciousness may actively reflect wisdom in thought, word, and deed. Man's outer-communication will reflect his inner level of consciousness. If the soul is in touch with its divine mental light consciousness, it will function as the "illumined soul-aware." Each one can actively seek and contact the place within in prayerful meditation.

In the stillness of self, man is able to touch into the "all knowing," guiding, Omniscient Source—the Divine Voice within. The inner voice becomes a directing force to channels of divine ideas, thoughts and truths to the enlightened one. The bloodstream of man unites with "spirit-stream." The dual being, the Gemini twin, consciously connects humanity with divinity; the two become one. The Gemini personal communicative intellect (Z rulership) illumines human mind to "Z" exaltation rulership, transcending, transforming, uniting,—full Light consciousness.

"And the cloud itself, which now before thee lies dark in view, shall with beams of light from inner glory be stricken through." Whittier

GOAL SUMMARIES

The exalted purpose of self is to consciously recognize, and purposely manifest ones divine inner Life Source and to elevate that Source in Joy!

CANCER—Emotional Will—foundation-heritage, protective, resourceful, keen memory, aware, sensitivity
Exaltation Ruler **"X"**
"X'—symbolic personal inner-desire presence, projected with purpose; to consciously express the nurturing, caring Source of being.

LEO—Spirit Love—new birth creation, outgoing, confident, strong, proud, radiant
Exaltation Ruler: **Pluto.**
Through Loves creative expression one may be "reborn", awakened to Spirit life fulfillment.

VIRGO—Physical Light—sensitive service, analytical, organized, industrious, discriminating
Exaltation Ruler: **Neptune**
Virgo exemplifies the physical fulfilling of self. Transforming, the "inner-light ideal"—purity of vision through discriminating service of thought, word and deed.

LIBRA—Mental Will—partnership-balance, refined, diplomatic, charming, idea-oriented, harmonious
Exaltation Ruler: **Uranus.**
To become consciously aware, realize freedom of individual Will, Individuality manifestation through balance in unity.

SCORPIO—Emotional Love—resourceful, responsible, loyal, intense, curious, possessive, patient
Exaltation Ruler: **Saturn.**
To demonstrate personality ego-sacrifice; development of deep personal worth, through fulfilling love responsibilities; to harvest (reap) life's and deaths hidden secrets.

SAGITTARIUS—Spirit Light—idealist, enthusiastic, truth seeking, philosopher, optimist, humorist
Exaltation Ruler: **Jupiter.**
To expand the Spirit Light of knowledge and truth teachings to inspired enlightenment.

CAPRICORN—Physical Will—public image goal projections, productive, traditional, dignified, practical
Exaltation Ruler: **Mars.**
To actively, openly, project and express Divine Will—To "Be" in purpose and manifestation

AQUARIUS—Mental Love—social humanitarian, promotes brotherhood, altruistic, charismatic

Exaltation Ruler: **Venus.**

To share, relate to others, from one's Omniscient Love Source, a detached Agape Love expression of harmony, beauty, and unity.

PISCES—Emotional Light—wisdom, idealistic beliefs and understandings, visionary, empathetic

Exaltation. Ruler: **Mercury.**

To receptively understand others, and impersonally communicate, reflect, one's benevolent beliefs of vision for the uplifting enlightenment of self and others.

ARIES—Spirit Will—self identity, "I AM"—personal projection, pioneer, individualistic, independent

Exaltation Ruler: **Sun.**

To personally fulfill the exalted state of self realization; a conscious recognition and application of one's divine identity.

TAURUS—Physical Love—security values, dependability, persistence, grounded, generous, loyal

Exaltation Ruler: **Moon.**

To personally expand, reflect and project one's "treasured possession values", one's inner-love security Source, to outer personality and physical manifestation

GEMINI—Mental Light—personal communicator, intellectual, gregarious, diverse, articulate, curious

Exaltation Ruler: **"Z".**

To consciously connect ones personal mind of intellect to one's intuitive "knowing" Omniscient Source; to personally function purposefully from one's inner guiding light.

ABOUT THE AUTHOR

Kay Andrews has held active memberships in astrological, philosophical, and metaphysical organizations for more than forty years. She is a past student of national and international astrologers and is presently a part-time teacher of astrology classes. Her ongoing avocation is for motivating and gratifying astrological self studies. She is also a practicing professional registered parliamentarian. Kay and her husband, Al, live in Litchfield Park, Arizona.